TRANSitions.
Transdisciplinary, Transmedial and Transnational
Cultural Studies
Transdisziplinäre, transmediale und transnationale
Studien zur Kultur

Volume / Band 13

Edited by / Herausgegeben von
Renata Dampc-Jarosz and / und Jadwiga Kita-Huber

Advisory Board / Wissenschaftlicher Beirat:
Lorella Bosco (University of Bari, Italy), Leszek Drong (University of Silesia, Poland), Elizabeth Duclos-Orsello (Salem State University, USA), Frank Ferguson (University of Ulster, Ireland), Odile Richard-Pauchet (University of Limoges, France), Monika Schmitz-Emans (University of Bochum, Germany), Władysław Witalisz (Jagiellonian University in Kraków, Poland)

The volumes of this series are peer-reviewed.
Die Bände dieser Reihe sind peer-reviewed.

Francesca Di Blasio / Maria Micaela Coppola /
Greta Perletti (eds.)

Always Connect

Transdisciplinarity and Intercultural Contact
in Literary Discourse

With 3 figures

V&R unipress

Bibliographic information published by the Deutsche Nationalbibliothek
The Deutsche Nationalbibliothek lists this publication in the Deutsche Nationalbibliografie;
detailed bibliographic data are available online: https://dnb.de.

The research leading to these results has received funding from the Department of Humanities of the University of Trento.

© 2024 by Brill | V&R unipress, Robert-Bosch-Breite 10, 37079 Göttingen, Germany,
an imprint of the Brill-Group
(Koninklijke Brill BV, Leiden, The Netherlands; Brill USA Inc., Boston MA, USA; Brill Asia Pte Ltd, Singapore; Brill Deutschland GmbH, Paderborn, Germany; Brill Österreich GmbH, Vienna, Austria)
Koninklijke Brill BV incorporates the imprints Brill, Brill Nijhoff, Brill Schöningh, Brill Fink, Brill mentis, Brill Wageningen Academic, Vandenhoeck & Ruprecht, Böhlau and V&R unipress.
All rights reserved. No part of this work may be reproduced or utilized in any form or by any means, electronic or mechanical, including photocopying, recording, or any information storage and retrieval system, without prior written permission from the publisher.

Cover image: Paul Klee, Tightrope Walker, 1923, The Cleveland Museum of Art. Creative Commons: Free Reuse (CC0).
Printed and bound by CPI books GmbH, Birkstraße 10, 25917 Leck, Germany
Printed in the EU.

Vandenhoeck & Ruprecht Verlage | www.vandenhoeck-ruprecht-verlage.com

ISSN 2751-8345
ISBN 978-3-8471-1744-5

Contents

Introduction 7

Bill Ashcroft (University of New South Wales)
Memory, Writing and Hope 13

Valérie Tosi (University of Pisa)
The 'Other-in-Self': Love, Ecological Interconnectedness, and
Socioemotional Vulnerability in Richard Flanagan's *The Living Sea of
Waking Dreams* 31

Francesca Di Blasio (University of Trento)
"Right us a wrong and break the thrall / That keeps us low". Indigenous
Australian Literature and Human Rights 47

Luca Pinelli (University of Bergamo & Université Sorbonne Nouvelle)
Of Monsters and Cannibals: Literature and the Body between Virginia
Woolf's Essays and Simone de Beauvoir's Philosophy and Literary
Theory 57

Silvia Purpuri (University of Trento)
The Welsh/English Tapestry. Bicultural Bilingualism in Dylan Thomas'
life and work 73

Paola Della Valle (University of Torino)
From Page to Screen: Undermining Nazi Propaganda in *Caging Skies* and
Jojo Rabbit 87

Chiara Polli (University of Messina)
Graphic Reportage across Languages and Cultures. A Translational
Perspective on Zerocalcare's Comics 99

Maria Festa (University of Torino)
Crossing Borders with the "Refugee Tales" Project 117

Paolo Caponi (University of Milano La Statale)
When Space Gets in the Way. The Suspension of Disbelief and "the best
quality of life possible" 131

Introduction

This volume examines the philosophical and scientific debate on cultural contact focusing on multidisciplinary and multiprospective approaches to literatures in English. Our title echoes the epigraph of E.M. Forster's novel, *Howards End* (1910 (2000)), one of if not his finest masterpiece. "Only connect", he writes, drawing our attention to the importance of making connections, a theme he returns to throughout the book. In many ways this novel prefigures the complexities and contradictions of the contemporary world, as it foreshadows a future of increasing urbanization, market logic, massification, and the difficulty of differentiating and cultivating both critical and emotional reflection. Only by continuing to make connections can we discover suitable representations of the real, and this volume invites us to rekindle and preserve our ability to connect.

The complexity of contemporary discourse with its myriad messages, codes, channels, and interlocutors, can only be addressed by preserving our capacity, again both critical and emotional, to create links and connections, and encouraging dialogue between the diverse solicitations that arise from the intricacies of reality. Literature, a device that simultaneously allows for emotional identification and cognitive projection, an artificer of emotive engagement and a promoter of critical thinking, plays a crucial role in this regard. And it is starting from literature that this volume traces the many possible connections that allow us to make our world interpretable consciously and in a convincing way.

Individuals and cultures are mutually involved in complex and protean dynamics. Multidisciplinary perspectives are essential to the representation and analysis of cultural phenomena. Thus, investigating the critical implications of such dynamics through a multidisciplinary literary lens which allows us to bridge the gaps between apparently divergent approaches is an increasingly relevant cultural and scholarly practice (Gurr & Kluwick 2021; Dossanovaa et Al. 2016). The main theoretical framework of this volume is broad yet specific: it spans a range of perspectives from cultural and postcolonial studies to anthropological, historical, juridical and philosophical reflections on cultural difference; it also includes theoretical views on the role of literature and the arts in both cooperative and conflictual cultural interactions in an age of "superdiversity".

In his contribution, Bill Ashcroft focuses on the relation between postcolonial writing and memory, arguing that the latter is a powerful resource because, despite the dangers of nostalgia, "it is not about recovering a past but about the production of possibility". Starting from Edouard Glissant's famous statement, "a prophetic vision of the past", Ashcroft argues that memory cannot only be a source of myth and record of historical contradictions and traumas, it can even show us the way forward, illuminating future action. Ashcroft investigates the connection between memory and the future by reflecting on the nature of time itself and provides a demonstration of circular time in postcolonial writing. Kamila Shamsie's *Kartography*, a text of cultural memory, is a case study that intertwines with Ernst Bloch's concept of utopian hope, for which art and literature are the pre-eminent vehicles. In fact, literature is capable of disseminating cultural memory because what we know about ourselves, our culture, our world, comes through stories.

Richard Flanagan's latest novel, *The Living Sea of Waking Dreams*, depicting an era of ecological crisis and social distancing, is analyzed through a psychological, philosophical, and ecocritical lens in Valerie Tosi's essay. Written during the Covid-19 pandemic, Flanagan's novel is a family drama about three middle-aged siblings who have to face their mother's ordeal with a lethal disease in the context of climate change and related environmental catastrophes. Tosi highlights how ecological issues are intertwined with postcolonial discourse and the personal histories of Flanagan's characters who experience alienation as both a psychological state and social phenomenon. Drawing on philosophical concepts such as ecophobia, ego- and eco-resiliency, multidirectional eco-memory, and on the eco-ontology framework developed by Roberto Marchesini, the author discusses how Flanagan creates a fictional world in which "the Other-in-Self" is key to preventing the physical and moral annihilation of the human.

Di Blasio's piece on Indigenous Australian literature reveals how an emotional juridical perspective can re-create a sense of cultural belonging by narrating Aboriginal versions of the Australian story. Her paper looks at the works of two writers, Oodgeroo Noonuccal and Kim Scott, who employ two different literary genres, poetry and fictional prose, focusing on the role literature can play in tackling the issue of Indigenous people's human and political rights. It is argued that literature functions as a metadiscoursive counterpart of any discourse on human rights, because it promotes the kind of critical understanding that enables us to distinguish merely 'legal' definitions from the varieties of meaning they take on in diverse human contexts. Di Blasio's contribution highlights "the close and yet not unequivocal ties" that connect human rights and social justice, and how emotions stirred by the aesthetics and ethics of literature can relate to this nexus.

Intercultural contact and philosophical views on [the experience of] the body are the main foci of Luca Pinelli's survey of Virginia Woolf and Simone de Beauvoir's theories on literature and the body. He emphasizes how literature is a continuously ritualized trade of embodied experiences. In "On Being Ill", Virginia Woolf famously stated that "literature does its best to maintain that its concern is with the mind; that the body is a sheet of plain glass through which the soul looks straight and clear, [that it] is dull, and negligible and non-existent. On the contrary, the very opposite is true". In a similar but perhaps more philosophical vein, Simone de Beauvoir argued in "Que peut la littérature?" that literature is a way of "overcoming separation by affirming it", that it is, as Proust maintained before her, it is the "privileged locus of intersubjectivity". Pinelli's paper creates a channel for communication between these two authors. He argues that a new view of literature emerges if we consider Woolf's description of the body as a "monster" and her oft-quoted idea of the novel as a "cannibal" alongside Beauvoir's philosophy, which looks at reading and writing as intercorporeal acts. Any approach that crosses different sorts of boundaries – national, disciplinary, generic – must emphasize the importance of the body of/in literature.

Silvia Purpuri's contribution explores the intricate linguistic and cultural duality of Welsh bilingual biculturalism, focusing on the life and work of the renowned Welsh poet, Dylan Thomas. Thomas was intimately tied to his Welsh roots but also embraced English influences. Purpuri explores how this interplay between Welsh and English languages and cultures shaped Thomas' life and creative expression, and fueled the enduring impact of his work, which foregrounds the unique dynamics of bicultural bilingualism in Welsh society. Providing a deeper understanding of the cultural and linguistic heritage that shaped Thomas' creativity, her paper sheds light on the broader implications of bicultural experience.

Any contemporary critical discourse on forms of inter-connection must address the interplay between novels and films, with their overt visual impact. Paola Della Valle focuses her study on the drama-comedy *Jojo Rabbit*, written and directed by Māori Taika Waititi who won the Oscar for best adapted screenplay in 2020. The film was inspired by Christine Leunens' bestselling novel *Caging Skies* and is also set in 1945 Nazi Germany. It shows the fall of Hitler through the eyes of a 10-year-old protagonist, Jojo, a Nazi fanatic, brainwashed by state propaganda. Della Valle demonstrates how the transition from literary text to film allows for unexpected alternative perspectives on one of the most dramatic periods in the history of the 20th century. Waititi's transgressive adaptation turns a serious topic into a parody that undermines power figures and power structures, leaving them open to ridicule. In so doing, it proves Brewer's point: that interdisciplinarity is 'the appropriate combination of knowledge from many different specialties – as a means to shed new light on an actual problem' (Brewer 1999, p. 329).

Chiara Polli's paper continues this exploration of the visual, looking at English translations of Zerocalcare's comic *Kobane Calling*. Polli first examines the intersection of comics and graphic reportage, the latter being one of the most accessible means for building socio-political awareness of the complexity of current events. The ninth art is often linked to this specific subgenre, as is the case with *Kobane Calling*. Translation is another element that must be considered in any critical discussion of cultural contact, and in this sense Polli's contribution stands at the crossroads of multiple discourses connecting text with text, source context with target context, and written communication with visual communication. She investigates textual forms that have resulted from contact between literary genres, with their multiple approaches to reality.

Continuing to consider alternative approaches to reality, Maria Festa's paper examines the role literature in the contemporary socio-cultural-anthropological scene, specifically in relation to the phenomenon of migration. Due to the proliferation and pervasiveness of new media, migrants' accounts often rely on multimodal media to relate on their journeys. Current technologies can also turn postcolonial literature into a fresh, diverse and at times hybrid act of narration, that engages readers in an interactive conversation with authors or addressers. The act of narrating may even take on a digital turn. Digital storytelling means authors no longer need to negotiate platforms to tell their stories; their voices can directly reach public spaces; narration can become a tool to advocate for a cause. Using this theoretical premise, Festa highlights the multi/inter/trans/disciplinary approaches to postcolonial literature evident in Reni Eddo-Lodge's *Why I'm No Longer Talking to White People about Race* and the "Refugee Tales Project". She shows how they are examples of hybridity "as a special mode or language of representation" (Paultz Moslund 2010, p. 4).

Paolo Caponi's contribution on narrative medicine, examines a recent study of great interest and equally great emotional intensity. A group in the medical team of the Istituto Nazionale dei Tumori in Milan has been experimenting with a new approach to terminally ill adolescent patients, encouraging them to project themselves onto alternative, different worlds or scenarios so as to detach themselves from their status quo. This palliative treatment can find its roots in Coleridge's speculative vision that poetry involves a "suspension of disbelief". By creating a benign vacuum in terms of their cognitive processing of their illness, these patients can attain "the best quality of life possible" (Clerici et Al. 2018) during the time they have left. In line with this vision, dreams they have during the terminal phase of illness are interpreted as movements towards auto-healing related to this "suspensive" approach to life and illness. Caponi focuses on this touching and affecting practical application of theory while addressing the general issue of recent developments in the Medical Humanities.

The further exploration of literature and its interactions with other disciplines such as history, philosophy, law, anthropology, the visual and multimedia arts, science and technology studies, the social sciences, and medicine, is promising. Such investigations can start from the field of literary discourse, while embracing multifarious multidisciplinary approaches. Literature can be seen as a complex and dynamic system, in which issues of cross-cultural contact can be tackled from different theoretical and methodological points of view. This volume examines the philosophical and scientific debate on cultural contact by investigating the critical implications of these dynamics through multidisciplinary perspectives within literary studies, and contributes to bridging the gap between apparently divergent approaches to texts, genres, genders, disciplines, media, theories, and cultures.

Francesca Di Blasio
Maria Micaela Coppola
Greta Perletti

Works Cited

Brewer, Garry D.: 'The Challenges of Interdisciplinarity', in: POLICY SCIENCES. The Theory and Practice of Interdisciplinary Work 1999/34, 4, pp. 327–337.

Dossanovaa Altynay Zh. et Al.: 'Interdisciplinary Approach to Understanding Literary Texts', in: INTERNATIONAL JOURNAL OF ENVIRONMENTAL & SCIENCE EDUCATION 2016/11, 10, pp. 3615–3629.

Forster, E.M.: Howards End [1910]. Penguin Classics, Harmondsworth 2000.

Gurr, Jens Martin / Kluwick Ursula: 'Literature and …? Perspectives on Interdisciplinarity', in: ANGLISTIK: INTERNATIONAL JOURNAL OF ENGLISH STUDIES 2021/32, 3, pp. 5–18.

Paultz Moslund, Sten: *Migration Literature and Hybridity: The Different Speeds of Transcultural Change*. Palgrave Macmillan, London 2010.

Bill Ashcroft (University of New South Wales)

Memory, Writing and Hope

In George Orwell's *1984* two things abolished by Big Brother were memory and writing. The intent of this is clear. Without memory we would no longer be fully human. Without memory we become robots. Memory is dangerous, not only because remembrance confirms our humanity, but because it's a reminder of what might be. In the postcolonial imagination, in particular, memory is not about recovering a past but about the production of possibility – memory enacted in postcolonial literatures is a recreation, not a looking backwards, but a reaching out to a horizon, somewhere 'out there'. This has been captured famously in Edouard Glissant's phrase, "a prophetic vision of the past," (1989: p. 64) a vision that informs all postcolonial writing. Postcolonial writing is dangerous, because it is the vehicle of cultural memory which enables vision of the future. In Ernst Bloch's terms the In-Front-Of-Us is always a possibility emerging from the past (1986: p. 4). In traditional postcolonial societies the radically New is always embedded in and transformed by the past.

While it runs the risk of nostalgia when a colonized society romanticizes a precolonial past, memory is a powerful tool available to the oppressed and marginalized. It is a source of myth, a recapitulation of historical contradictions and traumas, and a stimulus for future action. Myth may be positive or negative in the way it conceives cultural identity, but as history it is strategically placed to contest the ultimate imperial hegemony – history itself, which, as Chakrabarty claims, is always a version of the history of Europe (1992: p. 1). Nietzsche, in his essay "The Use and Abuse of History," discusses the usefulness of the quest for historical knowledge. On the one hand, too much engagement with history "mutilates and degrades lives" since it drains the vitality needed to build for the future. In this sense, "forgetfulness is a property of all action." But, on the other hand, the past, particularly "the monumental" past, is in his view one of the main sources of motivation for any great action. Thus, "the unhistorical and the historical" – forgetfulness and memory – are equally necessary to the health of an individual, a community and a system of culture." 'Historical men,' as Nietzsche calls them, are those who achieve an appropriate balance between the two: "Their vision of the past turns them towards the future…. They believe that the meaning of existence will become ever clearer in the course of its evolution; they look backward at the process only to understand the present and stimulate their longing for the future." In the postcolonial context, forgetting the experience of invasion but remembering its political reality is key to the hope for liberation.

While history, and its associated teleology, has been the means by which European concepts of time have been naturalized for colonized societies, the postcolonial re-conception of history is very clearly designed to "understand and stimulate their longing for the future" as Nietzsche puts it. For Edouard Glissant, "The past, to which we were subjected, which has not yet emerged as history for us, is, however, obsessively present" (1989: p. 54). A past which projects into the future, offers a prophetic vision. Such a vision, according to Glissant, is neither 'a schematic chronology' nor a 'nostalgic lament.' But ultimately its imagination, its hope for a future from the *past* is a critical strategy designed to resist the master discourse of History, a discourse from which Hegel notoriously excluded Africa in his "Introduction" to *The Philosophy of History*.

The conflict and disruption engendered by colonization have the potential to enhance creative work and writing is just one example of the insurgent creative power which refuses to be locked in to the status quo. The postcolonial situation stimulates change because the effect of colonial power is the *production* of hybridization and for Bhabha this is a positive (Bhabha 1994, p. 160). Writers writing from the in-between space of hybridization grapple at the same time with the challenges of identity formation, and with questions of place, nation and history. These writers envision renewal out of conflict, doing what Bhabha calls 'borderline work,' where conditions of displacement and disjunction have the potential to rewrite boundaries and borders, to reconceive the future in order to re-imagine the meaning of human community. This process deploys a radically transformed sense of the relation between memory and the future:

> The borderline work of culture demands an encounter with 'newness' that is not part of the continuum of past and present. It creates a sense of the new as an insurgent act of cultural translation. Such art does not merely recall the past as social cause or aesthetic precedent; it renews the past, re-figuring it as a contingent "in-between" space, that innovates and interrupts the performance of the present (Bhaba 1994, p. 10).

The very location of the future in the past establishes it as an "insurgent act of cultural translation." Thus, the postcolonial text in English can be understood as an insurgent transcultural act in which the writer and reader functions together produce a vision of the future.

Retrospective Future Thinking

While a prophetic vision of the past is a distinctive aspect of postcolonial narrative, a fascinating study by Roderer and Bonn demonstrates the way in which the past may be connected to the future for anyone. The study asked participants to imagine they were 100 years old and to reflect on the events they consider most important to their 100-year-old life. The authors discovered that "engaging in retrospective future thinking, taking a step forward in time and reflecting on one's life as if it has already been lived, provides several opportunities for investigating autobiographical events" (p. 23). But more importantly,

> retrospective future thinking enables a person to remember both past and future events as if these events had already been experienced – from a perspective that is more psychologically distant to the current self. This novel method allows examining the construction of both remembered and imagined autobiographical events in one paradigm, enabling the consideration of both theoretical and practical implications, for example for creating meaningful life narratives (p. 23).

Such an experiment demonstrates the ways in which the past may open up a particular kind of future. Although the subjects were asked to imagine future events, these were always based either on past experience or a sense of personal aptitude, interest and expectation. Future projections were guided by expectation inspired by past events. The (retrospective) future was envisaged in a combination of experience and hope and significantly, future hope was seen to be inextricable from the past. The beauty of such an experiment is that one could readily imagine it for oneself. Events seen from the perspective of my 100-year-old memory must be an extension of what I know to be possible from the experience of my past. This possibility lies at the very heart of creativity.

Memory is Performative

This study confirms that memory, like consciousness itself, is performative. It doesn't just happen, it is something that is done. If we think of memory as simply picturing the past we do well to consider Susan Sontag's discussion of the relationship between memory and photography:

> All memory is individual, unreproducible – it dies with each person. What is called collective memory is not a remembering but a stipulating: that this is important, and this is the story about how it happened, with the pictures that lock the story in our minds (Bertens 2020, p. 15).

This applies to all memory but is most prominently displayed in cultural memory:

> When applied to memory and remembrance performativity provides a framework for understanding the construction of memories. Like gender, memory has no fixed original which can be copied and passed on. For like gender, the construction of memory is not about the recreation of a historical truth, but is rather an answer to needs and desires in the present (Sontag 2003, p. 22).

The chequered history of eye-witness accounts confirms that there is no objectively correct memory; "each individual constructs memories, both personal and collective ones, by taking up elements of expressions of memories seen elsewhere and in turn expressing these. Even our own individual memories are not stable and every recounting of a memory in fact recreates and alters it slightly, according to the new context and purpose.

> On a cultural scale the performativity of memory means that each representation of a memory (in for instance film, literature, museums, oral history etc.) forms part of a dynamic and ongoing construction of that very memory (Bertens 2020, p. 186).

Writing produces cultural memory. But also writing, insofar as it is capable of producing unfamiliar and unstable perspectives and subjectivities, has the capacity to bring into presence that which is yet to exist, such is the function of the imagination. The poetic practice of writing trespasses the 'limits' of familiar and stable subjectivities viewpoints and voices and any relations that might exist actually or potentially between a reader and an author. "The unstable and unfamiliar is actively produced and changed in the process of writing and reading" (Agamben 1999, p. 68–9). Deleuze, following Nietzsche, notes that to create, one attends to forces not as 'form' but as being 'in a transformation' (1998, p. 105). The world's future in terms of its absolute potentiality, is immanent in our labour, our doing, creating and inventing. For Blanchot, "To write is to surrender to the interminable," and what is expressed in writing is "an absolute writing that no one writes: a potential to be written" (1982, p. 27).

Memory and Time

A full understanding of the capacity of the creative spirit to harness memory to anticipate the future requires close attention to the nature of time itself. Technically, the present doesn't actually exist, at least not in stasis, but is *always* a process of the future becoming past, anticipation becoming memory. To remember does not bring the past into the present, but the act of remembering or the invocation of memory transforms the fluid present. Memory refers to a past "that has never been present" not only because the present is a continual flow, but because memory invokes a past that must be *projected* so to speak, into the future, not only the future of its recalling, but the future of the realm of possibility itself. Put simply: "To speak of memory, is also to speak of the future."

The characteristic of Modernity with its concept of chronological 'empty' time, dislocated from place or human life separates past, present and future. Although the present may be seen as a continuous stream of prospections becoming retrospections, the sense that the past has gone and the future is coming separates what may be called the three phases of time. Friedrich Kummel proposes that the apparent conflict between time as succession and time as duration in philosophy comes about because we forget that time has no reality apart from the medium of human experience and thought (1968, p. 31). "No single and final definition of time is possible... since such a concept is always conditioned by man's understanding of it." (31) Or as Mahmoud Darwish puts it, "Time is a river / blurred by the tears we gaze through." (2002) Each moment is a flow of the past into the future. The present is the crucial site of the continual motion by which the New comes into being. Just as Roderer and Bonn found, memory is constantly connected to the future.

We think of time as either flowing or enduring but Kummel makes the point that duration without succession would lose all temporal characteristics. A theory of time therefore must understand the correlation of these two principles. Duration arises only from the stream of time and only within the background of duration is our awareness of succession possible. The critical consequence of this is that

> if something is to abide, endure, then its past may never be simply 'past,' but must in some way also remain "present" by the same token its future must already somehow be contained in its present. Duration is said to exist only when the "three times" (put in quotation marks when used in the sense of past, present and future) not only follow one another but are all at the same time conjointly present... the coexistence of the "times" means that a past time does not simply pass away to give way to a present time, but rather than both as *different* times may exist conjointly, even if not simultaneously (1968, pp. 35–36).

The present is the crucial site of the continual motion by which the New comes into being. One of the features of postcolonial texts, particularly those from Africa and the Caribbean, is a transformed conception of time that sees it as layered and interpenetrating rather than linear. This conjoining of time in these texts is related to a radically different epistemology – a different way of knowing.

All creative work makes this possible but writing, through its facility to produce narrative, has a particular relationship with time. The crucial characteristic of the genre of the novel, for instance, is its engagement with time. Stories are the way in which we have a world, and the telling of stories appeals to us because they offer the progress of a world in time and thus can become narratives of temporal order. But magically, by unfolding in time they take us out of time. It may be that narrative, whose materiality is isomorphic with temporality, provides a way (though not the only way) of communicating different experiences of time. How then can the novel convey a different knowledge of time, specifically knowledge of what has been called the 'broken' time of the traumatized colonized subject? One way of doing this is through the 'circular time' developed from the forms of oral story telling. But a more common way is to convey experience itself as a palimpsest of different phases of time and different orders of reality as Chinua Achebe does in a scene in which elders of the tribe perform the dance of the *egwugwu* or spirit beings, an occasion in which the ontological distinction between acting and reality, the human world and the spirit world, dissolves (1958, p. 85). Exactly the same laminating of time can be seen in the Aboriginal Dreaming, but it is more widespread than we realize. Salman Rushdie explains that the techniques of *Midnight's Children* reproduce the traditional techniques of the Indian oral narrative tradition going 'in great swoops, it goes in spirals or loops' rather than beginning, middle and end (Rushdie 1992, pp. 7–8).

This technique of circling back from the present to the past, its structure of building tale within tale, and its persistence in delaying climaxes are all features of traditional narration and orature. This oral technique is a way of articulating circular time, but in the postcolonial novel there is a further dimension, the circularity of the narrative is overlaid on an ontological circularity that revolves around the cultural disruption of colonialism. Emmanuel Eze to suggest that a prominent feature of the African novel is the presentation of 'broken' time. The African writer

> not only writes about African cultures as 'broken' by the experiences of colonialism but also appears to experience language itself – in this case, the language of writing – as re-enactment of otherwise de-centered traditions (2008, p. 25).
> It is as if in the writing, the writer historically inaugurates a different order of language and time, *a different sense of place* (p. 35).

On first consideration the idea of broken time, a brokenness that reflects the broken cultures of postcolonial African societies is persuasive. The colonial experience represents a moment of fracture between the traditional and the modern that is constantly negotiated in the language of the text. But it implies a culture that is a static object suddenly fractured and 'denatured' by colonialism, a fracturing that, just possibly, may be mended by a return to an essential cultural reality. This myth of return is common in postcolonial writing, but cultures are never static, they are always in process, in response to various historical influences. Without diminishing the traumatic historical event of colonialism and recognising the immense upheavals caused in African societies, the assumption of 'brokenness' underestimates the adaptability, the transformative power and *coeval* nature of African modernities. Although Eze uses the term 'broken' he has an astute sense of the way in which African writing captures the fluidity of culture

> on one level, postcolonial African writing is a language in movement: it is a language *in* time. On another level, however, just like the best of the modern African compositions in music, such a language, literally and figuratively, composes itself and its what [sic] in hiddenness: it is a language *of* the movement of time (p. 34).

It is a language in time because it is a transformed and appropriated English, but at the same time it is a language of time because African culture is deeply affected by the movement of time. This is not to say, however, that African time is 'broken' or that brokenness is the only way in which postcolonial time is known. Eze's main interest is in language but also in the way in which fiction operates in communicating the experience of time. The novel in particular, a form that hinges on temporal movement, is adept at communicating a different experience of time.

Postcolonial literatures continually affirm this sense of circular time, of the future in the past, and bring us back to our understanding of revolution as a revolving or spiralling into the future as well as a revolt against the failures of the past. The present is the crucial site of the continual motion by which the New comes into being. In such transformative conceptions of utopian hope, the future emerges from the past, not as nostalgia but as renewal. In traditional postcolonial societies the radically New is always embedded in and transformed by the past. For those Caribbean writers and artists working in the borderland of language, race, identity the past is the constant sign of the future.

Art, Literature and Cultural Memory

Cultural memory may not be *embodied* in individuals but *embedded* in much the same way as Anderson's concept of *Imagined Communities* embeds the concept of nation, in various kinds of texts. Indeed, we could say that

> literature is culture's memory, not as a simple recording device but as a body of commemorative actions that include the knowledge stored by a culture, and virtually all texts a culture has produced and by which a culture is constituted. Writing is both an act of memory and a new interpretation, by which every new text is etched into memory space (Lechman 2008, p. 301).

Such memory comes through the medium of stories, in whatever way the story is narrated. Tanzanian Sam Raiti Mtamba's puts it somewhat hyperbolically in his story "The Pound of Flesh":

... only art and literature could unlock the mysteries of life. Before men of letters there was nothing either cabalistic or magical. It was the open sesame, the sea into which everything flowed, the sea from which everything had its source and succor (2011, p. 167).

This is the euphoric outpouring of a man who wants to be a writer. Nigerian Chris Abani puts it more temperately in a talk on the stories of Africa:

What we know about how to be who we are comes from stories. It comes from the novels, the movies, the fashion magazines. It comes from popular culture. In other words it's the agents of our imagination who really shape who we are (2007a).

The imagination has the capacity to shape who we are by anticipating what we might become.

Paul Ricoeur's magisterial work, *Memory, History, Forgetting* argues the case for the political and moral imperative of remembrance. Despite the scope of the book, however, according to Suzi Adams (2019) Ricoeur did not address collective memory as cultural memory as articulated in Jan and Aleida Assmann's influential accounts (1995). The Assmanns cast cultural memory as a variety of collective memory that is embedded in social frames not embodied in human minds. Its sociality is irreducible to interaction and intersubjectivity. (112) For Ricoeur memory is a requirement of a self in order to exist; but cultural memory needs a living tradition and serves as a point of anchorage in a "tide of contradictory influences" that may come about through the various and possibly contradictory memories of individuals. Literary writing is a powerful way which cultural memory becomes embedded and its importance lies in its capacity to bring the embedded memory to mind. When the memory is articulated in literature it immediately prefigures future possibility.

Mythistory: Kamila Shamsie's *Kartography*

Kamila Shamsie's novel *Kartography* has been widely read as a document of cultural memory. It functions as a cautionary tale for the future. The historical consequences and trauma of Pakistan's 1971 war against Bangladesh are presented through fictional characters who personify various political, religious, and ethnic beliefs. Since *Kartography* fictionalises critical events in Pakistan's history and exploits characters as personifications, it qualifies as a mythistorical text (Liaqat and Mukhtar 2002, p. 156). The novel is set in Karachi city and chronicles the story of the two generations, recording the historical memories of postcolonial Pakistan by means of stereotyped characters. Set in 1971, and 1990, it narrates the history of four friends (Ali, Zafar, Yasmin, and Maheen) who belong to various provinces, races, and ethnicities of Pakistan. For instance, Zafar is a

Muhajir – someone who migrated to Pakistan after the Partition – and is engaged to Maheen, a Bengali, whereas Ali is a Punjabi and is engaged to Yasmin, a Pathan. The diversity of the group gestures towards a diverse future for Pakistan and "all the characters' narrative voices and perspectives stage the historical contingencies of Pakistan.

Zafar is a prototype for the Muhajir community, an ethnic division of those who migrated to Pakistan at the time of partition in 1947 and who are still considered allies of India, traitors, and outsiders in post-Partition Pakistan. Zafar represents this community and the prejudices the group faces in Pakistan still today (Shamsie 2002, p. 223). Similarly, Maheen represents the Bengali community, which was marginalised in the aftermath of the Partition (Shamsie 2002, pp. 42, 182, 183, 191, 232). Ali stands as a stereotypical Punjabi and Yasmin represents the Pathan community in Pakistan. Raheen epitomises the spirit of Pakistani Anglophone writers seeking to include marginalised voices of post-Partition Pakistan into the mainstream meta-discourse of Pakistani nationalism. Karim (Ali and Maheen's son) is a representative of the diasporic community of Pakistan, wanting to integrate a disintegrated post-Partition country into a cohesive map with all its singularities and diversities (Liaqat and Mukhtar 2002, p. 157).

Kartography's retelling of the tragic bloodshed of the 1971 civil war and ethnic riots of the 1990s in Pakistan is a cautionary projection into the future, implying the necessary corrective foreign and domestic policy changes needed for a more peaceful South Asian political environment. Many of the prejudices outlined in the novel still exist, fed on the ideas of religion, race, ethnicity, gender and political affiliation by providing insight into the cultural memories and identity politics of a postcolonial state where multiple ethnicities, races and groups are still trying to achieve stability it opens the way for future change. A novel such as *Kartography* projects into the future without seeming to, because it provides a warning about the political mistakes made on the basis of race, ethnicity and socio-economic division in a nascent postcolonial state. According to J&M,

> this novel also warns other postcolonial South Asian states to avoid ethnic, religious, sectarian and racial discrimination. It arguably implies the need for states to admit past mistakes rather than sweeping them under the proverbial rug, since – if they remain unresolved – these sensitive political issues will worsen relations in the South Asian region.

While novels such as *Kartography* act as a warning for the future, literary texts also open the path towards the future by giving voice to dreams of transformation.

Writing and Hope

At a rally in support of Salman Rushdie, Ben Okri made a statement that could almost have come from Ernst Bloch's *The Principle of Hope* so steeped is it in the anticipatory power of literature:

> Writers are amongst other things the dream mechanism of the human race. Fiction affects us the way dreams affect us. They share the same insubstantiality. They both have the capacity to alter reality. Dreams may be purer because they are not composed of words, but when fiction has entered into us, it no longer exists as words either. We can control our fictions to some extent, but we cannot control the effects that they have on the world and we can't wholly control our dreams (Okri 1990, p. 77).

For Bloch dreams are "a stepping stone to art..." (1986, p. 94) and the dream launches art beyond political commitment. As Caryl Phillips puts it, whatever the commitment or the politics of the writer his or her first commitment is to "write well".[1] Writing well means more than writing fluently, elegantly, or convincingly: it means writing in a way that realizes the full potential of the imagination. This is what launches the anticipatory consciousness of art and literature beyond the ideological environment of its production. "Literature as utopia is generally encroachment of the power of the imagination on new realities of experience" (Ueding 1978, p. 7). This is not, of course, to dismiss the revolutionary function of anti-colonial literature but to see this function as just the beginning of the political trajectory of postcolonial creative work. Seeing this is to more deeply understand 'revolution' itself.

For Bloch art and literature have a significant utopian function because their *raison d'être* is the imaging of a different world – what he calls their *Vorschein* or "anticipatory illumination". The anticipatory illumination is the revelation of the "possibilities for rearranging social and political relations to produce *Heimat*, Bloch's word for the *home* that we have all sensed but have never experienced or known.

"It is *Heimat* as utopia... that determines the truth content of a work of art" (Zipes 1988, p. xxxiii). *Heimat* becomes the utopian form in postcolonial writing that replaces the promise of nation.

As the home we have sensed but never experienced *Heimat* remains a constant beacon for the spirit of liberation even after the goals of colonial independence appear to have been achieved.

> What is envisioned as home (*Heimat*) in childhood is in actuality the goal of the upright gait toward which human beings strive as they seek to overcome exploitation, humiliation, oppression and disillusionment. The individual cannot attain such a goal, which

---

[1] Talk at EACLALS Conference, Venice, March 29th 2008.

is only possible as a collective enterprise. Yet the measure of the individual's ethical backbone can be determined by his or her struggle to stand and walk upright and contribute to the collective goal (Zipes 1988, p. xxvii).

The significance of the phrase "the upright gait" towards which human beings strive is that it identifies *Heimat* as the stimulus of a process rather than an identifiable goal. Indeed the individual may not be able to attain such a goal, but the collective enterprise, the sharing of the goal by writers and readers, may be achieved in art and literature.

One of the most common, and popular, examples of the performativity of cultural memory is the limbo dance, a performance of slave history, which re-enacts the crossing of the Middle Passage in a continual reminder of memory, survival and cultural resurrection. As Kamau Brathwaite puts it,

> Limbo
> Limbo like me
> Long dark deck and the water surrounding me
> Long dark deck and the silence is over me (Brathwaite 1969, p. 35).

The dancer goes under the limbo stick in an almost impossible bodily position, emulating the subjection of the slave body in the journey across the Atlantic but rising triumphant on the other side. The performance of memory is a constant reminder of a future horizon, a 'return' that performs each time the 'rising' of the slave body into a future marked not only by survival but also by renewal, hybridity and hope. The dance is a metaphor of slave history that celebrates the present with the continuous re-enactment of future hope.

So past present and future are conjoined in the creative work in a radical transformation of the reality of slave exile. The descendants of the slave labour of sugar plantations have developed a culture that draws its ontological energy from the very fact of displacement, of homelessness, heterogeneity and syncreticity. This is a form of revolution as transformation, but its relation to time is exactly the same as that on which revolution depends, because the revolt is also a re-volving, an evolution in which past present and future are conjoined and mutually enforcing. In the case of the African novel for instance, what Emmanuel Eze sees as the 'fractured time' of colonial experience is in fact a layering of past present and future. Kummel sees this relation between past present and future as a feature of all human life so that "the openness of future and past is, in other words, the vital condition for the conduct of man's life and all his actions" (50). We make the past our own by bringing it into a free and positive relation with the present. "The natural discrepancy of future and past constitutes a productive tension, which forms the real medium for new action and new mediation" (50). In other words, the tension of revolution is rendered productive by its location in a spiraling compression of time.

The Limbo dance, while a performance of the journey across the Middle passage and a triumphant emergence into a transformed future, demonstrates the distinction between individual and collective memory. Individuals performing the dance might have no thought about its origins or meaning, but when it is recapitulated in narrative and poetry the broader cultural significance becomes clearer.

Literature is particularly strategic in the production of cultural memory. "Memory and processes of remembering have always been important and dominant topics in literature" (Neumann 2008, p. 333). Literature contributes to the larger discussion of the ways in which societies recollect their past. Even more than this,

> literature is culture's memory, not as a simple recording device but as a body of commemorative actions that include the knowledge stored by a culture, and virtually all texts a culture has produced and by which a culture is constituted. Writing is both an act of memory and a new interpretation, by which every new text is etched into memory space (Lechman 2008, p. 301).

Of course, literature's role is not limited to record keeping. It interprets existing memories and literary texts also act as 'Relay stations... stabilisers... Catalysts... Objects of recollection... [and] Calibrators' (Rigney 2008, pp. 350–351) of collective memory. In fact, literature 'forms an important part of...cultural repertoire' (Burke 2017, p. 20).

The contingency of the past disrupts the apparent polarity between past and future and for Ernst Bloch this disruption is absolutely necessary to understand the nature of the relationship between being and possibility. He asserts that for Plato 'Beingness' is 'Beenness' (1984, p. 8) and he admonishes Hegel because "What Has Been overwhelms what is approaching... the categories Future, Front, Novum" (p. 8). The problem with the concept of Being in Hegel was that it overwhelmed *becoming* – obstructing the category of the future. It is only when the static concept of being is dispensed with that the real dimension of hope opens (p. 18). The core of Bloch's ontology is that 'Beingness' is 'Not-Yet-Becomeness':

> Thus the Not-Yet-Conscious in man belongs completely to the Not-Yet-Become, Not-Yet-Brought-Out, Manifested-Out in the world... From the anticipatory, therefore, knowledge is to be gained on the basis of an ontology of the Not-Yet (p. 13).

While utopias exist in the future, utopianism, anticipatory consciousness, is heavily invested in the present. In Bloch's re-interpretation of Marx his ontology of becoming has a political, liberatory dimension. The energy of the masses in the German (1525), French and Russian revolutions "were attracted and illuminated by a real future place: by the realm of freedom" (p. 143). Bloch's cyclic theory is of the future in the past and this is a characteristic he allocates to Marxist philosophy itself (p. 9).

A very clear example of this can be found in the strategic use of a postcard called "Visit Palestine." designed in 1936 by Franz Kraus.

Fig. 1

This operates as an iconic point of connection between past present and future. The postcard embeds memory by identifying Palestine as a destination – an actual identifiable place in the world before the Nakba – and out of the reality of the country as a destination emerges the utopian concept of destiny. The postcard operates as a hinge between past present and future by becoming a palimpsest. The past is present in Amer Shomali's *Visit* in which the wall testifies to the attempt by the state of Israel to not just incarcerate the Palestinians but to wall off the past (see Fig. 2).

For Palestinians the original *Visit Palestine* published by the Tourist Development Association of Palestine in 1936 has come to be seen as an iconic reminder of their historical presence in the Holy Land. This image of the past drives the Palestinian view of a separate and liberated state in the future.

Fig. 2

Time, Utopia and Utopianism

A central feature of postcolonial narrative is the prevalence of change and transformation, the hope for a different future. Such a vision of a different world that suffuses all postcolonial writing can be called utopian. The importance of a perception of time in which past present and future are conjoined or layered rather than separate and lost to each other is that it refutes one of the most trenchant critiques of utopia – its static nature. The assumption is that although utopias lie in the future, representations of them, particularly those in the transcendental utopian tradition, suggest that they cannot progress. Indeed, for Bloch there is a very important difference between utopias and utopianism. His insistence on the centrality of the utopian to human consciousness, and the magisterial way in which *The Principle of Hope* outlines the operation of *utopianism* as a fundamental feature of human life perhaps explains his central importance to utopian theory:

> Primarily, everybody lives in the future, because they strive… Function and content of hope are experienced continuously, and in times of rising societies [revolutions] they have been continuously activated and extended (Bloch 1986, p. 4).

Bloch urges us to grasp the three dimensions of human temporality: he offers us a dialectical analysis of the *past* which illuminates the *present* and can direct us to a better *future*. This reformulation of time privileges the ongoing function of utopianism over abstract utopias. Bloch's major premise is the energizing of the present with the anticipation of what is to come. This is what Mahmoud Darwish sees as the *saturation* of the present and future in the past.

But can utopianism exist without a vision of utopia? What the Visit Palestine postcard series reveals is that *Heimat* is not Paradise. Home is not the 'non-place' – Utopia – nor is home the shimmering object in the distance. Home is the luminous possibility of the present and in this respect it is far from static, but a dynamic horizon of everyday living. Freedom, like consciousness, can never exist in the abstract, it must be realised in the terms 'freedom from' and 'freedom to'. But even further than this, freedom can only exist in the act of struggle against coercion, 'freedom to' may only be realised in the struggle of 'freedom from' domination and the transformation of power. In Palestine, the utopian impulse revolves around the reality of a place – but the utopian is enacted in the engagement with power. The vision of utopia is located in the act of transformation of coercive power, a certain kind of *praxis* rather than a specific mode of representation.

We see this in Larissa Sansour's vision of a Palestine as a skyscraper, a single estate (see Fig. 3).

The pun on 'living the high life' captures the possibility of a different kind of Palestine. What this image demonstrates in the way in which cultural memory can be embedded and can open the path to a different future.

We can test the grounded nature of *Nation Estate* by comparing it to another of Sansour's pieces: the short film called *Space Exodus* which shows a Palestinian female astronaut planting a Palestinian flag on the moon. This not "grounded," in the way that *Nation Estate* is grounded in the reality of Palestinian dispossession and renewal of the past, yet neither is it utopia. *Space Exodus* is a representation of what appears to be the impossible. But it demonstrates precisely how the utopianism of art and literature work. By the very act of representing the impossible, the work clears a space for the imagination. It may be improbable but the very production of the film contests its impossibility. In this way memory opens a pathway to hope through the medium of literary writing.

Fig. 3

Works Cited

Achebe, Chinua: Things Fall Apart. Heinemann, London 1958.
Adams, Suzi: 'A Note on Ricoeur's Early Notion of Cultural Memory', in: Études Ricoeuriennes / Ricoeur Studies 10/1, pp. 112–124.
Agamben, Giorgio: Potentialities: Collected Essays in Philosophy (ed. and trans. D. Heller-Roazen). Stanford University, Press Stanford 1999.
Assmann, Jan: 'Collective Memory and Cultural Identity'. In: New German Critique, 1995/65, pp. 125–33.
Bertens, Laura M.F.: "Doing' Memory: Performativity and Cultural Memory in Janet Cardiff and George Bures Miller's Alter Bahnhof Video Walk', in: Holocaust Studies, 2020/26, 2, pp. 181–197.
Bhabha, Homi: The Location of Culture. Routledge, London 1994.
Blanchot, Maurice: The Space of Literature (trans. A. Smock). University of Nebraska Press, Lincoln, NE and London 1982.
Bloch, Ernst: *The Principle of Hope* 3 vols (trans. Neville Plaice, Stephen Plaice and Paul Knight). University of Minnesota Press, Minneapolis 1986.

Brathwaite, Edward Kamau: Islands. Oxford University Press, London1969.
Burke, Peter: 'Shaping Memories in Literature and Cultural Memory', in: Herbert Grabes / Mihaela Irimia / Andreea Paris / Dragos Manea (eds.): *Literature and Cultural Memory*, Brill, Leiden 2017, pp. 19–30.
Chakrabarty, Dipesh, 'Postcoloniality and the Artifice of History: Who Speaks for "Indian" Pasts?', in: REPRESENTATIONS (Berkeley, Calif.), 1992/37, 37, p. 1–26.
Deleuze, Gilles: Essays Critical and Clinical (trans. D.W. Smith and M.A. Greco). Verso, London and New York 1998.
Eze, Emmanuel Chukwudi: 'Language and Time in Post-colonial Experience', in: RESEARCH IN AFRICAN LITERATURES 2008/39, 1, pp. 24–47.
Glissant, Edouard: *Caribbean Discourse: Selected Essays* (trans. with introd. by J. Michael Dash). University Press of Virginia, Charlottesville 1989.
Kummel, Friedrich: 'Time as Succession and the Problem of Duration', in J.T. Fraser (ed.): *The Voices of Time*. Allen Lane, London 1968.
Lechman, Renate: 'Mnemonic and Intertextual Aspects of Literature', in: Astrid Erll / Aßnsgar Nünning (eds.): *Media and Cultural Memory*, Walter de Gruyter GmbH & Co. Berlin 2008, pp. 301–310.
Liaqat, Qurratulaen / Asia Mukhtar: 'Poetics and Politics of Postpartition Cultural Memories in Kamila Shamsie's Kartography', in: CONTEMPORARY SOUTH ASIA 2022/30:2, pp. 154–165.
Mtamba, Sam Raita: 'Areas of Shade, Areas of Darkness. Poems and Stories', in: Gordon Collier (ed.): *Spheres Public and Private: Western Genres in African Literature* (*Matatu* 39). Rodopi, Amsterdam and New York 2011.
Okri, Ben: 'Statements at Conference Organized by the Institute of Contemporary Arts, London: Ben Okri, Maggie Gee, Farrukh Dhondy, Anon., Malise Ruthven, Marina Warner', in: CARDOZO STUDIES IN LAW AND LITERATURE, 1990/2, 1, pp. 77–89.
Ricoeur, Paul: Memory, History, Forgetting. University of Chicago Press, Chicago 2004.
Rigney, Ann: 'The Dynamics of Remembrance: Texts Between Monumentality and Morphing', in: Astrid Erll / Aßnsgar Nünning (eds.): *Media and Cultural Memory*. Walter de Gruyter GmbH & Co. Berlin 2008, pp. 345–356.
Roderer, Ayleen / Annette Bohn: 'Retrospective Future Thinking as a Novel Method to Imagine the Future: Remembering Autobiographical Events from the Perspective of the Future Self', in: MEMORY, 2023/31, 1, pp. 22–33.
Rushdie, Salman: Imaginary Homelands: Essays and Criticism 1981–1991. Granta, London 1992.
Shamsie, Kamila: Kartography. Oxford University Press. Karachi 2002.
Sontag, Susan: Regarding the Pain of Others. Picador, New York 2003.
Ueding, Gert: 'Literatur ist Utopie', in: Gert Ueding (ed.): *Literatur ist Utopie*. Suhrkamp, Frankfurt am Main 1978.
Zipes, Jack: 'Introduction: Toward a Realization of Anticipatory Illumination', in: Ernst Bloch, *The Utopian Function of Art and Literature: Selected Essays* (trans. Jack Zipes and Frank Mecklenburg). University of Minnesota Press Minneapolis 1988.

Websources

Abani, Chris: Chris Abani on the stories of Africa (TED) (2007) http://www.ted.com/talks/chris_abani_on_the_stories_of_africa.html (Accessed July 2003).

Darwish, Mahmoud: A State of Siege (2002) http://www.arabworldbooks.com/Literature/poetry4.html (Accessed November 2003).

Valérie Tosi (University of Pisa)

The 'Other-in-Self': Love, Ecological Interconnectedness, and Socioemotional Vulnerability in Richard Flanagan's *The Living Sea of Waking Dreams*

Just before the spread of the Covid-19 pandemics, from the 1st of July 2019 to the 31st of March 2020, unprecedented heath storms sparked massive bushfires that scorched millions of acres from the outback regions to the Australian and Tasmanian coasts. During this period, which has been labelled 'the Australian Black Summer', thirty-four people were killed by the wildfires. Furthermore, experts estimated the death and displacement of rare and threatened animal, plant, and insect species whose loss is now believed to be permanent.

Against this apocalyptic background Flanagan sets *The Living Sea of Waking Dreams* (2020), which lies at the intersection of family novel, psychological fiction, *ecoliterature*, and the fantastic genre. Since the plot revolves around dysfunctional family relationships and patterns of feelings in an era of climate crisis and social media tyranny, the reader is led to classify the novel as (eco-)psychological realism. However, the trope of the vanishing body is a vessel for the *Unheimlich*, which enters the narrative unsettling the reader.

In this article I intend to investigate how Flanagan combines the fantastic mode with discourses pertaining to scientific and humanistic disciplines such as ecology, philosophy, psychology, and anthropology to represent a world on the verge of an ecological, emotional, social, and ethical apocalypse. Furthermore, I will discuss how the novel 'cries' for ecological awareness and cognitive change. It's my view that the author, dramatizing the obsolescence of the Anthropocene's epistemological and ontological paradigms through the interplay of characters and the narratological device of reported thought, highlights the need for a new eco-ontology akin to the model developed by Roberto Marchesini.

In *The Living Sea of Waking Dreams* Tasmania's bushfires are the backdrop of a family drama which develops around the dying of Francis, an 86-year-old woman suffering from cancer. When she is admitted to a Hobart's hospital as a terminally ill patient, her children are summoned to her bedside: there is Anna, a famous middle-aged architect who is in a relationship with a woman and has a son with a mental illness; Terzo, a wealthy trader whose self-confidence and egocentrism border on control freakiness; and Tommy, a poor and failed artist with a stutter that appeared after he was abused at a Marist Fathers' boarding school. Anna and Terzo are "joined by an unspoken guilt" (Flanagan 2020, p. 37), since Tommy is the only one who has taken care of their mother while they were egoistically pursuing their career paths in Sydney and Brisbane. They feel offended when Tommy, "the most bourgeois of embarrassments: the lower-class relative" (p. 40–41) states that they should let Francie die, because their money makes them feel entitled to defy the laws of nature and keep their mother alive.

Running parallel to this realistic narrative is an uncanny story about bodily vanishings. As Anna is increasingly involved in her mother's care planning, as she gradually becomes aware of her son Gus's sociopathy, and as she repeatedly experiences parental and eco-anxiety, she starts to lose body parts. One day, while looking for a parking space in front of the Hobart hospital, she looks at her left hand and is able to count only the thumb and three fingers:

> Between her little finger and her middle finger, where her ring finger had once connected to her hand, there was now a diffuse light, a blurring of the knuckle joint, the effect not unlike the photoshopping of problematic faces, hips, thighs, wrinkles and sundry deformities, with some truth or other blurred out of the picture [...] There was no pain. There was no immediate sense of ache or loss. There was just a vanishing. (p. 15)

The vanishing of Anna's finger is depicted by comparing this inexplicable phenomenon to a photoshop effect. In this passage Flanagan mentions a 'blurring of truth' related to the digital alteration of a body image, perhaps hinting at the detrimental effects of our 'liquid' society's fear of aging, obsession with beauty standards, and "pursuit of fitness" (Bauman 2000, p. 78), which may erase our personal history and somatic identity. The narrator tells us that Anna "had certain rules about her life. One was that she didn't get sick. Another was that she refused to surrender to age. [...] She was ashamed to learn that she was old" (Flanagan 2020, p. 196–197). However, what happens to Anna's body plays into a more ecocultural form of Anthropocene anxiety. Anna's ring finger, a knee, a hand, and a breast vanish one after the other in the same way many species of her world are dying out from cataclysmic events or human interference.

Anna's ongoing vanishing can be read on two metaphorical levels, pertaining to sociopsychological and ecological issues respectively. Considering her body both as a psychological, social and affective construct, a "mind-brain-body" (Dodds 2013), I argue that Anna's disappearing may be read as a representation of her self-detachment and socioemotional disconnection. Since the beginning of the novel, she feels "something going" (Flanagan 2020, p. 7), but she is not able to identify that void as a result of her emotional disability. She just sees others "staring at her as if she were a ghost, or mad, or both, a mad ghost" (p. 46), since "nobody noticed, nothing changed, all that was lost remained unfound" (p. 131). From this perspective, the physical vanishing serves as a metaphor for emotional neglect, relating the human body to those feelings of emptiness and nonexistence that lots of people must cope with in today's individualist society. Her altered perception of her body could be seen as a symptom of a psychological disorder akin to depersonalization and derealization[1], which are dissociative disorders often caused by traumagenic events such as abuses, losses, incidents, wars, pandemics, and environmental catastrophes. Her brother Ronnie's suicide, the challenging health conditions of her mother, her family disruption, the lack of mutual love and esteem between Anna and her brothers, and her emotionally sterile relationship with Meg lead her to depression, anxiety and a sense of invisibility that degenerates into hallucination. Furthermore, her state anxiety and self-detachment are worsened by the environmental degradation and disasters she daily observes through her phone screen. One day, after checking the news feed and reading various pieces on mass extinction, "she ran a finger around the side of her chest [...] *and then*...nothing" (p. 149, emphasis in original). When she realises a breast is vanished, she feels panicked. However, her distress is soon replaced by a sort of "dispassionate, almost detached interest" (p. 151) that runs parallel with her social alienation.

When her ring finger vanishes, Anna's *Ego-resiliency* manifests itself as a foolish fantasy beyond the mask of rationality. *Ego-resiliency* is a dynamic capacity which systematically modifies control, optimizing the personality system with regards to the environmental context[2]. Anna states that "Getting old was simply about losing so many things: hearing, teeth, sight, sense, and no, she guessed, body parts. Perhaps it wasn't that strange" (Flanagan 2020, p. 47). At first, her Ego-control is put under pressure by the vanishing, but soon she accepts it as something ordinary in the social and environmental dystopia in which she is immersed. A few days later, when her left knee and a second finger disappear, she feels as if drunk, but "instead of thinking, instead of feeling, she frantically searched *missing fingers* on her phone" (p. 141), looking for a rational explanation to her fading away. Since she realises that no one sees her as a suffering human being, and therefore no one can notice her missing parts, she resigns herself to her extraordinary condition, swiping to news feed on her smartphone. Faced with the global dimension of bushfires, "a politician was saying they shouldn't waste another word talking about climate change but simply adapt and be more resilient" (ibid.). In this passage Flanagan introduces the philosophic concept of resilience relating it with politics. Anna's *Ego-resiliency* reveals itself to be influenced by the Governance, which denaturalises the principle of resil-

---

[1] Depersonalization/derealization disorder is a type of dissociative disorder that consists of persistent or recurrent feelings of being detached from one's body or mental processes (depersonalization), or from one's surroundings (derealization). See Lynn et al 2012; Gatus et al. 2022.
[2] See Block, Jeanne / Block, Jack 1980.

ience turning it into a controllable, almost rational, adaptive behaviour. "Were they adapting to their own extinction?" (ibid.) Anna asks herself, suggesting how imposed resilience may result in fatalism and inaction. Drawing a parallel between *Eco-resiliency*[3] and *Ego-resiliency* in a world undergoing a process of extinction, Flanagan leads the reader to reflect upon the cognitive and emotional aspects of ecological consciousness, as well as on human responsibility on climate crisis. From an eco-psychological and eco-affective perspective, Anna's altered mental status can be analysed as a form of post-traumatic stress disorder caused by the perception of impending ecological threats that affect her body as well as the environment. At the beginning of the novel, the narrator reports Anna's thought: "It's impossible to say how the vanishing began [...] Whether it's about me or her or him, whether it's she or we or you, whether it's now or then or soon" (p. 3), and forty pages later, we read that "the way she had not memory of its vanishing, that was what was traumatic" (p. 45). Anna's vanishing becomes apparent in a dramatic ecological moment, characterised by wildfires spread everywhere and a smoke that "enclosed the world in a way that felt claustrophobic", an "acrid, tarry, sulphurous smoke that burnt the back of every throat and filled every mouth and nose blocking out the warm gentle smells of summer" (p. 13). Placing a vanishing human body within the dying body of Australia, Flanagan draws on the notion of trauma to express Anna's inner condition and her relationship with time, space, and other human beings. It's my point that the author presents an ecological view of Anna's psychoemotional trauma that recalls certain assumptions of applied social psychology about the Australian Black Summer.

A vast body of work on the interaction between climate change and mental health has emerged in the last ten years. According to psychologists, mental health outcomes of climate change range from minimal distress symptoms to clinical disorders, such as anxiety, depression, post-traumatic stress, alterations in perception, and suicidal thoughts[4]. Studies performed in Australian areas hit by bushfires observed that a year after the events 42% (n = 1,526) of the victims exposed was classified as potential psychiatric cases. Their psychological condition was analysed through The General Health Questionnaire (GHQ) and the Anxiety, Affective and Post-Traumatic Stress Disorder modules of the Diagnostic

---

3 In 1973, Canadian ecologist Crawford. S. Holling proposed to consider the behaviour of ecological systems "in terms of the probability of extinction of their elements, and by shifting emphasis from the equilibrium states to the conditions for persistence" (Holling 1973, p. 2). Therefore, he introduced the word 'resilience' into the ecological literature as a way of helping to understand the non-linear dynamics observed in ecosystems. *Eco-resiliency* was defined as the amount of disturbance that an ecosystem could withstand without changing self-organized processes and structures.

4 See Ursano et al. 2017; Hayes et al. 2018, Chique et al. 2021.

Interview Schedule (DIS). Post-disaster mental health issues observed were post-traumatic stress disorder, psychological hyperarousal, chronic dissociation, sadness, depression, *solastalgia*[5], detachment, disorganized thinking and behaviour, numbing or avoidance, poor concentration, and behavioural problems[6]. Drawing on psychological studies and eco-psychological theory, we could maintain that Anna's vanishing is a kind of cognitive distortion, namely a symptom of a depersonalization-derealisation disorder that makes her perceive her body as visually unfamiliar. Past and recent research findings have revealed the relationship between derealization, depersonalisation and aversive, anomalous body processes or body-threats related to natural and anthropogenic disasters[7].

Anna's body is also readable as an "ecological threshold [own translation]" (Marchesini 2018, p. 130). From the perspective of affective ecology, human-nature connections are produced through an interactivity of mind, body, and environment[8]. Furthermore, how we relate to the environment is not only a cognitive and aesthetic affair since connectedness with nature entails an emotional dimension. According to Bladow and Ladino, "Bodies, human and non-human, are perhaps the most salient sites at which affect and ecocriticism come together" (Bladow and Ladino 2018, p. 3). In Flanagan's novel, Anna is emotionally detached from the natural environment as well as she is from her family, while her brother Tommy, who is shocked by the fact that many Tasmanian insects, plants, and birds are facing extinction, is "aware of a growing scream that was within him and outside him" (Flanagan 2020, p. 4) and feels "a pain [...] a sickness growing within him" (p. 7). When faced with the dispiriting prospect of her dying mother, the specter of the wildfire devastation that threatens Tasmania, the thought of her son Gus, and the vanishing that is erasing her body, Anna feels psychologically and emotionally overwhelmed, and disappears into Instagram and Facebook to find some relief from a harsh reality. However, this distraction technique reveals itself to be ineffective, since it triggers further confusion, anxiety, and sense of helplessness.

---

5 In *The Living Sea of Waking Dreams* Flanagan provides a definition of *solastalgia* as "emotion induced by the loss of everything" (Flanagan 2020, p. 103). The term *solastalgia* was coined by Australian philosopher Glenn Albrecht in 2005 to define "the pain or sickness caused by the loss or lack of solace and the sense of isolation connected to the present state of one's home and territory" (Albrecht 2005, p. 44).
6 See Bryant et al. 2021; Chique et al. 2021; Cowlishaw et al. 2021; Crandon et al. 2022, Zhang et al. 2022.
7 See Noyes and Kletty 1977; Dewe et al. 2016; Canan and North 2019; Naushad et al. 2019.
8 See Zylstra et al. 2014; Cooke et al. 2016; Pramova et al. 2022.

The following passages are representative of how the author represents hyperinformation, contradictory information, and the palimpsestic nature of information in the era of climate crisis and social media tyranny:

> She drifted into her social media. An article on herbal remedies for anxiety. On new bathroom trends. On a town about to run dry that had all its remained water granted to a coal mining company. Posts of friends travelling. Whitegoods clothes shoes cosmetics conspiracies a farmer tweeting how kangaroos kept lying in his front garden and dying drought is a bushfire in slow motion, he wrote. Like share update friends subscribe. (p. 21)

> She looked at her phone she checked Instagram she read professors of health were calling for cities to be readied for mass evacuation Indigenous people fearing central Australia is becoming too hot for humans towns running out of water Australia ending its hottest year ever while someone was saying it wasn't, that official weather records had been forged to make Australia look colder in the past and hotter now. (p. 87)

In a recent interview published in *The Guardian*, Flanagan maintained that social media abuse results in social disconnection and escapism. In his view, nowadays people tend to live "through a world reified back to them through a small screen and its madness" (Flanagan / Williams 2020), overlooking or intentionally disregarding serious matters such as global conflicts and the contemporary ecological crisis. In *The Living Sea of Waking Dreams*, environmental information mediated by social media contributes to leading characters to *ecophobia*[9], a feeling of powerlessness to prevent natural cataclysms and anthropogenic disasters that often results in fear, indifference, or even ecological denial. Anna is representative of this psycho-affective pathological condition. Feeling overwhelmed by the impending bushfires that threaten Hobart, she turns to social media to dispel her eco-anxiety. However, misinformation, biased information, and overlapping information make her unable to distinguish between factual reality, political and sociocultural constructs, and mere fantasies. So, she is stuck in a state of non-feeling, numbness, and apathy that make her feel powerless and vulnerable:

> A world burning and nothing bringing it back. It was possible to feel nothing it was necessary to feel nothing, the news feeds and social media feeds made you feel absolutely nothing: she could do nothing she would do nothing she was nothing. That was good. Other than keep her mother alive as everything died, nothing. She would flush the toilet she would watch the world die let her mother live nothing nothing nothing. (Flanagan 2020, p. 98)

---

9 In *The Ecophobia Hypothesis* (2018) Simon C. Estok describes *ecophobia* as "a uniquely human psychological condition that prompts antipathy toward nature" and that can embody "fear, contempt, indifference, or lack of mindfulness (Estok 2018, p. 1).

In 2011 Robert Gifford, professor of Psychology and Environmental Studies at the University of Victoria (Canada), presented a table of seven psychological barriers that limit climate change mitigation and adaptation; among those, *environmental numbness* stands out as a form of limited cognition often related to the way environmental concerns are articulated by the media[10]. Mentioning George E. Belch, Marian K. Burke, and Julie A. Edell's research in cognitive psychology, Gifford argues that "when viewers have seen the same advertisement many times, attention to it shrinks as habituation increases" (ibid.). Similarly, Slovic and Slovic have pointed out that some people react to overwhelming data such as reports of high fire danger, record temperatures, melting glaciers, and threatened species with "psychic numbing" (Slovic / Slovic 2015, p. 2).

In his fictional world, Flanagan offers us various representations of the psychological barriers identified by Gifford, showing us, for example, how *judgmental discounting*[11] is a cognitive strategy people adopt to deny evidence, avoid responsibility, and blame others for climate change-related catastrophes. Anna reports on the adoption of this strategy, maintaining that 'when the first famines began, they were elsewhere, and the growing numbers of wars were elsewhere, and elsewhere is always the fault of others (Flanagan 2020, p. 233-234). When Anna's brother Terzo is struck by a truck and killed during a bike racing, Anna attends his funeral, where she finds herself standing in a circle of venture capitalists who complain about time-consuming bureaucratic regulations on environmental and financial issues. She describes their talk focusing on the incomprehensible language they speak: 'they talked fin-ech and ag-tech and ed-tech law-tach reg-tech and tech-tech. A rounds and B rounds and down rounds, LPs and floats and phoenixes until finally returning to green tape red so the song cycle could begin again' (p. 219). The insistence on the prefix 'tech-' recalls Gifford's notion of *technosalvation*[12] as one of the ideologies of the Anthropocene and one of the main psychological barriers to climate-change awareness. In Flanagan's novel, *technosalvation*, strictly connected to *system justification*[13], deeply orients the way people think, behave, and interact. The language spoken by Terzo's colleagues is onomatopoetically related to *techne*, showing how "techno-mediation" (Marchesini 2017, p. 143) affect both content and form of the

---

10 Gifford relates *environmental numbness* to selective information processing, frequency of information, and redundant information (see Gifford 2011, p. 292).
11 *Judgmental discounting* means "undervaluing of distant of future risks" as well as the "rationalization for a variety of deviant behaviours, the goal of which is to absolve oneself from responsibility" (Gifford 2011, p. 292-293).
12 *Technosalvation* is a form of cognitive dissonance resulting in the belief that technology alone can fix all current ecological and social problems (see Gifford 2011, p. 293).
13 Gifford defines *system justification* as "the tendency to defend and justify the societal status quo" (Gifford 2011, p. 293).

communication processes. While talking with a young entrepreneur at Terzo's funeral, Anna is astonished by his automaton-like behaviour, since "he seemed to reboot as if he had found the appropriate information in some remote cloud server" (Flanagan 2020, p. 221). Terzo's colleagues are represented as mere machines processing information without any emotional involvement. Behaving and speaking like computers, they show how "technopoiesis increases the human hybridization by introjecting the non-human existential dimensions reached with a techno-mediation" (Marchesini 2017, p. 143). However, this form of hybridization has its drawbacks, since "they no longer knew how to talk with their children or their parents and perhaps never had, that they were lost, or alone" (Flanagan 2020, p. 220) and "no one could any longer decide what was sickness and what was health, what was living and what was dying, far less know what was good and evil" (p. 221).

In Flanagan's novel this ideology of *technosalvation* reflects also in the way human beings insist on prolonging individual lives, "completely autistic to the widespread death of all the life [...] that actually supports life" (Flanagan / Kaplan 2021). Anna's mother is dehumanised and turned into a futuristic machine through medical technology:

> Francie's body, now little more than skin clutching the sticks of her bones, was not that of a frail old animal but an intricate twenty-first century machine that could be kept working with the body's technicians and engineers ceaselessly oiling, replacing, lubricating and fuelling its various mechanical parts. (Flanagan 2020, p. 95)

It is Anna and Terzo's will, "coupled to the formidable technology that will could summon to its aid" (p. 211) that turns their mother into a "marionette suspended by tubes" (p. 247), and "tested in extremis" (p. 248). *Environmental numbness, judgmental discounting, system justification* and *technosalvation* have both social and affective implications, since they result in mistrust, suspicion, scapegoating, therapeutic obstinacy, and emotional blunting. Anna knows that therapeutic obstinacy is a nonsensical form of violence, and at a certain point she seems to become aware of her own cruelty, feeling that "to inflict such a torment in a sentient creature in any other sphere of life would be considered criminally psychopathic and merit heavy punishment" (p. 246). However, she neutralises her cognitive dissonance pretending she is merely obeying her brother Terzo's will to keep their mother alive, and replacing emotional empathy with calculated pity, a form of "lie", "vanity" and "sorrow grounded in the illusion of power" (p. 246–247).

From an ecological perspective, Anna's progressive vanishing can be interpreted as a metonym of a real and broader vanishing occurring in her world, since the whole natural environment around her is burning. Through this lens, Flanagan's novel could be read as a speculative narrative that uses fantastic elements to depict a world dying out in slow motion. According to Gifford, for many citizens climate change is "a phenomenon outside immediate attention because it is not causing any immediate personal difficulties" (Gifford 2011, p. 292). Flanagan expresses the same idea by drawing a parallelism human body and the earth's body. Anna doesn't care for the fantastic phenomenon of vanishing until she realises that she misses the erased parts of her body, and that the vanishing process is unstoppable and widespread: her son, her doctor, her girlfriend, and finally all the people around her are vanishing, as well as meaningful human interactions and the social order. The whole of mankind has either vanished or turned into cyclops-like creatures unable to take their eyes off their smartphones. These monsters can be read as a metaphor of human egotism, lack of empathy, and digital slavery. However, they could also be interpreted as fantastic beings, a mutant specimen generated by an affective devolution of human beings. At the end of the novel, Anna herself will realise that she has undergone this horrifying metamorphosis, and that she has only one eye left in the middle of her forehead.

Before the situation spirals out of control, on one of her flights home from Hobart to Sydney, Anna becomes acquainted with Lisa Shahn, a scientist who runs a government program to save the Australian orange-bellied parrot. While chatting, Lisa tells Anna the story of Mathinna, an Indigenous girl stolen from her family by the whites – the arctic explorer Sir John Franklin and his wife – and then abandoned and left to die. Lisa relates the attempted extermination of Mathinna's people to other catastrophes that turn out to be less natural than anthropogenic:

> Mathinna's people burnt the plains and kept the mosaic of plains and forest alive, the tiny parrots ate the seeds and sedges of the wet plains [...] But when the Aboriginals lost the war and the few survivors were taken away by the burning stopped, the forest advanced, the plains began vanishing and he seeds and sedges with them, and the birds started their long vanishing also. But nothing ever really vanishes. Does it? Massacring Mathinna's people, the plains, the seeds and the sedges. The beauty. The birds. (Flanagan 2020, p. 189)

Then Lisa tells Anna the story her Lithuanian grandmother, who survived to the Holocaust thanks to the aid of a compassionate policeman, and points out that "Maybe [...] her grandmother was just another Mathinna" (p. 190). Three chapters before the narrator mentioned the term *omnicide*[14] (p. 103) as one of the new words used to describe the age of climate change, hinting at an intrinsic

---

14 The term *omnicide* was coined by American philosopher John Somerville in his article 'Einstein's Legacy and Nuclear Omnicide' (1986), where he defined omnicide as "the terminal extension of the series of existing words which denote types and quantitative ranges of the killing of human beings" (Somerville 1986, p. 24).

interaction between natural disasters and human action. The term *omnicide* echoes the logic of destruction on a mass scale, anticipating the issue of Jewish and Indigenous mass murder discussed by Lisa. Basing on Michael Rothberg's notion of *multidirectional memory* (2009) and Rosanne Kennedy's concept of *multidirectional eco-memory* (2017), I argue that in this novel Flanagan draws connections between historical and ecological catastrophes, bringing "histories of the decline and resilience of human and animal populations" (Kennedy 2017, p. 268) into a literary frame. Rothberg describes *multidirectional memory* as a way of conceptualizing what happens when different histories of extreme violence confront each other in the public sphere. In his view, collective memory, far from being 'competitive', is "multicultural" and "*multidirectional*, as subject to ongoing negotiation, cross-referencing, and borrowing; as productive and not privative" (Rothberg 2009, p. 3, emphasis in original). Multidirectional memory "encourages us to think of the public sphere as a malleable discursive space in which groups do not simply articulate established positions but actually come into being through their dialogical interactions with others" (p. 5). Lisa's story shocks Anna, who "felt a confusion rising like a riot" (Flanagan 2020, p. 188), having to cope with an uncomfortable 'national past' and opening to another culture's *affiliative*[15] structures, namely Indigenous knowledge, history, and memory.

Furthermore, Flanagan sheds light on the ecological interconnection between Indigenous identity and Country. Lisa explains to Anna that "Early white explorers described the Aboriginals' camps [...] *as if sited with an aesthetic eye. Not they were. No. As if*" (p. 191, emphasis in original). Perhaps drawing on historical, philosophical, and ecological considerations expressed by Bruce Pascoe's in *Dark Emu. Black Seeds, Agriculture or Accident* (2014), Flanagan gives voice to Indigenous memory challenging the Western-centric and imperialistic paradigm of *terra nullius*[16], and identifies indigenous group identity as an ecological and affective interconnectedness based on mutual nurturing.

Kennedy defines *eco-memory* as "a deep memory of a habitat, conceived as an ecological assemblage in which all elements, human and nonhuman, are mobile, connected, and interactive" (Kennedy 2017, p. 269), and argues that "it is compatible with an Indigenous conception of 'country'" (ibid.). Hence, her elaboration of *multidirectional eco-memory:* "Multidirectional eco-memory places

---

15 By *filiation*, Said means the writer's natural connection with inherited tradition, while *affiliation* is a network of relationships that human beings make consciously through social and intercultural exchange (see Said 20–21).
16 *Terra nullius* – land belonging to nobody – is a Latin expression derived from the Roman expression res nullius – a thing belonging to no one – by analogy (see Benton and Strauman, qtd. in Ashcroft, B. / Griffiths, G. / Tiffin, H. 2003, p. 257). Coined in the nineteenth century, the term was commonly used to depict the colonists' attitude in Australia.

memories of the violence against and dispossession of particular human populations in complex, nuanced relation to memories of the suffering, slaughter, and endangerment of animal populations" (ibid.). In Flanagan's novel, *multidirectional eco-memory* informs Lisa's attitude towards her ecocultural world when she states that "Maybe the birds were her Mathinnas" (Flanagan 2020, p. 191), but it's Anna that finally identifies the affective nature of the contemporary ecological crisis: "The more the thought about it the more she wondered if maybe that's what humans can do. Live with beauty. That it's beauty they can't bear. That what was really vanishing wasn't all the birds and fish and animals and plants, but love" (ibid.).

After losing her loved ones and being turned into a one-eyed creature, Anna decides to seek relief from her horrifying everyday reality. Therefore, she joins Lisa Shahn' team and flies to Port Davey. There she helps a group of volunteers to count how many orange-bellied parrots are arriving to lay eggs. However, while checking an empty nest, she has a heart attack. Before dying, she has a sort of revelatory dream, in which she goes through various metamorphoses: a gum tree, a Tasmanian tigress, a wedged-tailed eagle, a crayfish, a Tasmanian devil, a specimen of myrtle, pencil pine, richea, and scoparia. In each metamorphosis she is the last of her species until she turns into a primordial organism without further possibility of regeneration. It's only when she becomes embodied in other living beings and experiences *ecocide*[17] at an accelerated pace, that she realises that the world is facing extinction because of human beings' incapacity to see and love its wonderful beauty. Anna points out that people "had not been expelled from Eden [...] they had expelled Eden from themselves and there would be no return" (p. 274). The narrator reports her "environmental epiphany" (Vining / Merrick 2012) as a revision of the position of the human in the ecological dimension:

> She had grown up, she realised too late, in the autumn of things, an extraordinary world – its ancient rainforests, its wild rivers, its beaches and oceans, its birds and animals and fish, all were to her a path to freedom and transcendence, and none – she only now saw – were but a transitory wonder so soon to vanish until all that remained for a short time longer were human beings. But just for a short time. They could not survive alone, outside of the wonder – what could? – and so that time too would end. (Flanagan 2020, p. 275)

---

[17] The word *ecocide* was first recorded at the Conference on war and national responsibility in Washington in 1970, where American plant biologist and bioethicist Arthur Galston used this term to describe the environmental harm inflicted upon South Vietnam by defoliation and bombing. Galston was the first to link the international crime of genocide to a crime committed against nature.

In this passage, Flanagan hints at a new way of conceiving the human-nature relationship that echoes the concept of 'new gentleness' developed by Neil Campbell. Drawing on Félix Guattari's *Les trois écologies* (1989), Campbell identifies 'new gentleness' as a mix of curiosity, wonder, attunement, and ethical responsibility that would enable a re-valuing of the local as a powerful means to appreciate the everyday and the overlooked as vital elements within a more inclusive understanding of how we live[18]. The depiction of the orange-bellied parrot at the end of the novel is reminiscent of this idea of curiosity, wonder, and care as triggers for a local *ecosophic*[19] activism. After admiring "the tiny bird, green as hope, newly arrived, two tiny eyes brilliant as balls of dropped ink" (Flanagan 2020, p. 281) Lisa Shahn sees the "immense gift, the intense gratitude" (p. 282) for living in a still beautiful world and feels "ready" (282) to carry on her mission.

In *Eco-ontologia. L'essere umano come relazione* (2018), Marchesini argues that the Self needs to be "dispersed in the other" and "nourish through others [own translation]" (p.17) to validate itself. He identifies this condition as "ontologic heterotrophy [own translation]" (ibid.), developing his eco-ontology as a relational ontology based on openness, curiosity, interconnectedness, and care ethics. Proposing a replacement of the philosophical concept 'Other-than-the-Self' with a new notion of "Other-in-the-Self [own translation]" (p. 27), Marchesini claims for a new posthumanist framework that he identifies as relational humanism. From his perspective, human beings should see themselves as crossable thresholds, body-mind constructs that are open to the wonder of encounters. Drawing on his idea of human life as a process of "somatization of relations [own translation]" (p. 25) and "epiphanies generated by the encounter with the Other-in-the Self [own translation]" (p. 28), I maintain that Anna's revelatory dream represents her coming to terms with the Other-in-the-Self's beauty and vulnerability through a crossing of her cognitive and affective Self. Through an imaginative projection into other vanished or vanishing living beings, Anna experiences disorientation, fear, anguish, and grief, realizing, only at the end of her own life, that she has always been part of the ecological world she and the most of mankind see as 'Other-than-the-Self'.

In this article I highlighted how *The Living Sea of Waking Dreams* deals with psychological, anthropological, philosophical, and environmental issues that

---

18 See Campbell 2018.
19 The term *ecosophy* was coined in 1973 by the Norwegian philosopher Arne Naess to identify "a philosophy of harmony with nature or ecological balance" (Naess 1973, p. 124). Drawing on Naess' notion of *ecosophy*, the French psychoanalyst, poststructuralist philosopher, and political activist Félix Guattari developed a philosophical ecology consisting in the articulation of three registers: environmental, social, and psychological. In *Les Trois Écologies* he called this interaction *écosophie* (Guattari 1989, p. 12).

pertain to current debates at the core of various scientific disciplines and humanities. I discussed how concepts and notions drawn from environmental philosophy and socioecological psychology might be useful for reading the novel's fictional world, as a "more realistic than metaphorical" (Flanagan / Kaplan 2021) mirror of our own world. Conversely, I have underlined how this novel makes contemporary and important issues accessible to readers that are not familiar with environmental studies. Flanagan's novel is representative of a new kind of *ecoliterature* that challenges what Amitav Ghosh has identified as a "crisis of culture, and thus of the imagination" (Ghosh 2016, p. 9) in the face of global warming and environmental catastrophes. In fact, it draws unexpected connections between environmental and human vulnerability, identifying affection as the key to social and ecological survival.

Discussing his novel in a recent interview with Kaplan, Flanagan has maintained that he does not feel responsible for conveying moral or political messages through his fiction. He has pointed out that while journalists are 'responsible' for what they say, authors are allowed to be 'irresponsible'. In his view, novels, free from political constraints, are more powerful than nonfiction to awaken consciousness in unexpected ways and touch deeper chords in the soul, since they are inherently based on cognitive, emotional, and spiritual connections that go beyond cultural differences and ideological bias. The salvific nature of fiction lies therefore in its being able to feed the imagination, elicit wonder and promote empathetic identification with the Otherness that exists in the Self.

I conclude my article by quoting Flanagan's own words, which express this idea of literature as a tool for re-framing our being-in-the-world within an eco-affective paradigm:

> Writing this book I realized that it remains such a beautiful world. If we can just see the world for what it is and what it offers we would not give up on it. So much blinds us: novels are one form that can help restore a necessary sense of wonder and, with it, humility and gratitude. (Flanagan / Parsons 2021)

Works Cited

Albrecht, Glenn: 'Solastalgia, a New Concept in Human Health and Identity', in: Philosophy Activism Nature 2005/3, p. 41–55, available at: https://doi.org/10.1080/10398560701701288 [24/03/2022].

Ashcroft, Bill / Griffiths, Gareth / Tiffin, Helen: Postcolonial Studies. The Key Concepts. Routledge, New York 2003.

Bauman, Zygmunt: Liquid Modernity. Polity Press, Cambdridge, UK 2000.

Bladow, Kyle / Ladino, Jennifer: Affective Ecocriticism. Emotion, Embodiment, Environment. University of Nebraska Press, Lincoln 2018.

Block, Jeanne / Block, Jack: 'The Role of Ego-control and Ego-resiliency in the Organization of Behavior', in Collins, Andrew W. (ed.): *Development of Cognition, Affect and Social Relations: The Minnesota Symposia on Child Psychology*, L. Erlbaum Associates, Hillsdale, NJ 1980, p. 39–101.

Bryant, Richard A. / Gibbs, Lisa / Gallagher, Colin H. / Pattison, Phillipa / Lusher, Dean / MacDougall, Colin / Harms, Louise / Block, Karen / Ireton, Greg / Richardson, John / Forbes, David / Molyneaux, Robyn / O'Donnell, Meaghan: 'The Dynamic Course of Psychological Outcomes Following the Victorian Black Saturday Bushfires', in: AUSTRALIAN AND NEW ZEALAND JOURNAL OF PSYCHIATRY 2021/7, p. 666–677, available at: https://doi.org/10.1177/0004867420969815 [24/03/2022].

Campbell, Neil: 'A New Gentleness: Affective Ficto-regionality', in Bladow, Kyle / Ladino, Jennifer (eds.): *Affective Ecocriticism. Emotion, Embodiment, Environment.* University of Nebraska Press, Lincoln 2018, p. 71–92.

Canan, Fatih / North, Carol S.: 'Dissociation and Disasters: A Systematic Review', in: WORLD JOURNAL OF PSYCHIATRY 2019/6, p. 83–98, available at: https://doi.org/10.5498/wjp.v9.i6.83 [24/03/2022].

Chique, Carlos / Hynds, Paul D. / Nyhan, Marguerite M. / Lambert, Sharon / Boudou, Martin / O'Dwyer, Jean: 'Psychological Impairment and Extreme Weather Event (EWE) Exposure, 1980–2020: A Global Pooled Analysis Integrating Mental Health and Wellbeing Metrics', in: INTERNATIONAL JOURNAL OF HYGIENE AND ENVIRONMENTAL HEALTH 2021/238, available at: https://doi.org/10.1016/j.ijheh.2021.113840 [24/03/2022].

Cooke, Benjamin / West, Simon / Boonstra, Wiebren. J.: 'Dwelling in the Biosphere: Exploring an Embodied Human-environment Connection in Resilience Thinking', in: SUSTAINABILITY SCIENCE 2016/5, p. 831–843, available at: https://doi.org/10.1007/s11625-016-0367-3 [24/03/2022].

Cowlishaw, Sean / Metcalf, Olivia / Varker, Tracey / Stone, Caleb / Molyneaux, Robyn / Gibbs, Lisa / Block, Karen / Harms, Louise / MacDougall, Colin / Gallagher, Colin H. / Bryant, Richard A. / Lawrence-Wood, Ellie / Kellett, Connie / O'Donnell, Meaghan / Forbes, David: 'Anger Dimensions and Mental Health Following a Disaster: Distribution and Implications After a Major Bushfire', in: JOURNAL OF TRAUMATIC STRESS 2021/1, p. 46–55, available at: https://doi.org/10.1002/jts.22616 [24/03/2022].

Crandon, Tara J. / Dey, Cybele / Scott, James G. / Thomas, Anna J. / Ali, Suhailah / Charlson, Fiona J.: 'The Clinical implications of Climate Change for Mental Health', in: NATURE HUMAN BEHAVIOUR 2022/6, available at: https://doi.org/10.1038/s41562-022-01477-6 [24/03/2022].

Dewe, Hayley / Watson, Derrick G. / Braithwaite Jason J.: 'Uncomfortably Numb: New Evidence for Suppressed Emotional Reactivity in Response to Body-threats in Those Predisposed to Sub-clinical Dissociative Experiences', in: COGNITIVE NEUROPSYCHIATRY 2016/5, p. 377–401, available at https://doi.org/10.1080/13546805.2016.1212703 [24/03/2022].

Dodds, Joseph. 'Minding the Ecological Body: Neuropsychoanalysis and Ecopsychoanalysis', in: FRONTIERS IN PSYCHOLOGY 2013/4, available at: https://doi.org/10.3389/fpsyg.2013.00125 [24/03/2022].

Estok, Simon: The Ecophobia Hypothesis. Routledge, New York 2018.

Flanagan, Richard: The Living Sea of Waking Dreams. Chatto & Windus, London 2020.

Flanagan, Richard / Williams, Michael: 'Despair is Always Rational, But Hope is Human', in THE GUARDIAN, 2020, available at: https://www.theguardian.com/books/2020/sep/29/richard-flanagan-despair-is-always-rational-but-hope-is-human [24/03/2022].

Flanagan, Richard / Parsons, Cherilyn: 'Richard Flanagan: What the Writer Needs is a Mad Courage', in: LITERARY HUB, 2021, available at: https://lithub.com/richard-flanagan-what-the-writer-needs-is-a-mad-courage/ [24/03/2022].

Flanagan, Richard / Kaplan, Mitchell: 'Richard Flanagan on Writing (and Rewriting) Through the Devastating Bushfires in Tasmania and Australia', in: LITERARY LIFE PODCAST, 2021, available at: https://lithub.com/richard-flanagan-on-writing-and-rewriting-through-the-devastating-bushfires-in-tasmania-and-australia/ [24/03/2022].

Gatus, Andrew / Jamieson, Graham / Stevenson, Bruce: 'Past and Future Explanations for Depersonalization and Derealization Disorder: A Role for Predictive Coding', in: FRONTIERS IN HUMAN NEUROSCIENCE 2022/16, available at: https://doi.org/10.3389%2Ffnhum.2022.744487 [24/03/2022].

Ghosh, Amitav: The Great Derangement: Climate Change and the Unthinkable. The University of Chicago Press, Chicago 2016.

Gifford, Robert: 'The Dragons of Inaction: Psychological Barriers That Limit Climate Change Mitigation and Adaptation', in: AMERICAN PSYCHOLOGIST 2011/4, p. 290–302.

Guattari, Félix: Les trois écologies. Galilée, Paris 1989.

Hayes, Katie / Blashki, Grant / Wiseman, John / Burke, Susie / Reifels, Lennart: 'Climate Change and Mental Health: Risks, Impacts and Priority Actions', in: INTERNATIONAL JOURNAL OF MENTAL HEALTH SYSTEMS 2018/12, available at: https://doi.org/10.1186/s13033-018-0210-6 [24/03/2022].

Holling, Crawford S.: 'Resilience and Stability of Ecological System's', in: ANNUAL REVIEW OF ECOLOGY AND SYSTEMATICS, 1973, p. 1–23, available at: http://www.jstor.org/stable/2096802 [24/03/2022].

Kennedy, Rosanne: 'Multidirectional Eco-memory in an Era of Extinction', in: Heise, Ursula / Christensen, John Niemann; Michelle (eds.): *The Routledge Companion to Environmental Humanities*, Routledge, London/New York 2017, p. 268–277.

Kolev, Ognyan I., Georgieva-Zhostova, Spaska O. / Berthoz, Alain: 'Anxiety Changes Depersonalization and Derealization Symptoms in Vestibular Patients', in: BEHAVIOURAL NEUROLOGY, 2014, available at: https://doi.org/10.1155/2014/847054 [24/03/2022].

Lynn, Steven J. / Lilienfled, Scott O. / Merckelbach, Harald / Giesbrecht, Timo / Van Der Kloet, Dalena: 'Dissociation and Dissociative Disorders: Challenging Conventional Wisdom', in: CURRENT DIRECTIONS IN PSYCHOLOGICAL SCIENCE 2012/1, p. 48–53, available at: https://doi.org/10.1177/0963721411429457 [24/03/2022].

Marchesini, Roberto: Eco-ontologia. L'essere come relazione. Apeiron, Napoli 2018.

Marchesini, Roberto: Over the Human. Post-humanism and the Concept of Animal Epiphany. Springer, Cham 2017.

Naess, Aarne: 'Deep ecology', in: Merchant, Carolyn (ed.): *Key Concepts in Critical Theory: Ecology*, Atlantic Highlands, NJ 1994, p. 120–124.

Naushad, Vamanjore A. / Bierens, Joost J. L. M. / Nishan, Kunnummel P. / Firjeeth, Chirakkal P. / Mohammad, Osama H. / Maliyakkal, Abdul M. / Chalihadan, Sajid / Schreiber, Merritt D.: 'A Systematic Review of the Impact of Disaster on the Mental Health of Medical Responders', in: PREHOSPITAL AND DISASTER MEDICINE, 2019/6, p. 632–643, available at: https://doi.org/10.1017/S1049023X19004874 [24/03/2022].

Pramova, Emilia / Locatelli, Bruno / Valdivia-Díaz, Merelyn / Vallet, Améline / Quispe Conde, Yésica / Houria, Djoudi / Colloff, Matthew J. / Bousquet, François / Tassin, Jacques / Munera Roldan, Claudia: 'Sensing, Feeling, Thinking: Relating to Nature With the Body, Heart and Mind', in: PEOPLE AND NATURE 2022/2, p. 351–364, available at: https://doi.org/10.1002/pan3.10286 [24/03/2022].

Rothberg, Michael: *Multidirectional Memory: Remembering the Holocaust in the Age of Decolonization*. Stanford University Press, Stanford 2009.

Russell Noyes / Kletti Roy: 'Depersonalization in Response to Life-threatening Danger', in: COMPREHENSIVE PSYCHIATRY 1977/4, p. 375–384, available at: https://doi.org/10.1016/0010-440X(77)90010-4 [24/03/2022].

Said, Edward: The World, The Text, and The Critic. Harvard University Press, Cambridge, MA 1983.

Slovic, Scott / Slovic Paul: Numbers and Nerves. Information, Emotion, and Meaning in a World of Data. Oregon State University, Corvallis 2015.

Somerville, John: 'Einstein's Legacy and Nuclear Omnicide', in: PEACE RESEARCH 1986/1, p. 20–58, available at: http://www.jstor.org/stable/23609711 [24/03/2022].

Ursano, Robert J. / Morganstein, Joshua C. / Cooper, Robin: American Psychiatric Association Position Statement on Mental Health and Climate Change. 2018, available at: https://www.psychiatry.org/File%20Library/Psychiatrists/Directories/Library-and-Archive/resource_documents/2017-Resource-Document-Mental-Health-Climate-Change.pdf [24/03/2022].

Vining, Joanne / Merrick, Melinda S.: 'Environmental Epiphanies: Theoretical Foundations and Practical Applications', in: Clayton, Susan D. (ed.): *The Oxford Handbook of Environmental and Conservation Psychology*, 2012, available at: https://doi.org/10.1093/oxfordhb/9780199733026.013.0026 [24/03/2022].

Zhang, Yanqin / Workman, Annabelle / Russell, Melissa A. / Williamson, Michelle / Pan, Haotai / Reifels, Lennart: 'The long-term impact of bushfires on the mental health of Australians: a systematic review and meta-analysis', in: EUROPEAN JOURNAL OF PSYCHOTRAUMATOLOGY, 2022, available at: https://doi.org/10.1080/20008198.2022.2087980 [24/03/2022].

Zylstra, Matthew J. / Knight, Andrew / Esler, Karen J. / Le Grange, Lesley L. L.: 'Connectedness as a Core Conservation Concern: An Interdisciplinary Review of Theory and a Call for Practice', in: SPRINGER SCIENCE REVIEWS, 2014/1–2, p. 119–143, available at: https://doi.org/10.1007/s40362-014-0021-3 [24/03/2022].

Francesca Di Blasio (University of Trento)

"Right us a wrong and break the thrall / That keeps us low". Indigenous Australian Literature and Human Rights

The ethical, metaethical and political function of literature

In the current debate on the formidable potential of interdisciplinarity in literary studies, the issue of human rights is of particular relevance. In fact, it directly addresses the socio-political power of literature as an instrument of knowledge, a feature that other interdisciplinary approaches tend to overlook or at least downplay. I argue here that literature functions as the metadiscoursive counterpart of any discourse on human rights, promoting the critical understanding that enables us to distinguish merely 'legal' definitions from the varieties of meaning they take on in diverse human contexts. Just consider the title Brenda Carr Vellino chose for her paper on human rights pedagogy in Canadian schools: 'Everything I Know about Human Rights I Learned from Literature' (Carr Vellino 2004, p. 135). This title echoes, in a light-hearted and humorous way, the philosophical position expounded by Percy Bysshe Shelley in his *A Defense of Poetry* in the early nineteenth century. The *Defense* is in many ways one of the foundational texts of contemporary discourse on ethics and literature, the core issue addressed here, and one I return to below.

A full discussion of the relationship between literature and human rights would require a great deal of time, and I recognize that the case study chosen for this discussion, *i.e.*, contemporary Indigenous Australian literature, would benefit from a broader introduction. In this paper, however, introductory yet representative remarks will be provided on both subjects. Despite notable strides Indigenous Studies made over the last decade or two not only in the Australian context, Aboriginal literature still occupies a relatively niche position in the current cultural debate. I will deal with a few paradigmatic elements from selected texts that belong to different literary genres and historical moments ranging from the 1960s to the present day. More specifically, there will be two main foci. I first consider the "poetemics" of Oodgeroo of the tribe Noonuccal, poetemics being Mudrooroo Narogin's portmanteau which blends "poetry" with "polemics" to highlight the political stance Oodgeroo takes in her poetic production, her insistence on tackling [issues related to] the pervasive racism and negation of the human and civil rights of Indigenous people in Australia during the 1960s. Oodgeroo Noonuccal, aka Kath Walker, an Indigenous poet and activist who passed away in 1993, was the first Aboriginal author to publish a collection of poetry in 1964. I next turn to consider Kim Scott's fiction. Scott, a contemporary Noongar writer who has been awarded or shortlisted for several important literary prizes (twice winner of the Miles Franklin Literary Award), authored, among others, a trilogy of novels depicting different phases of Australian colonial and postcolonial history. He highlights the political relevance and systematic denial of various fundamental human and civil rights using a form of fiction that intersects with documentary history.

The issue of human rights involves considerable complexity, but offers substantial insight into multifarious situations that literature is typically able to represent through both mimesis and projection (Locatelli 2002, p. 23). The reverse though is also true: precisely thanks to the cognitive and representational power of literature, which always touches on ethical, emotional, and aesthetic issues, it plays an important role in the conception and development of any discourse on human rights, as Goldberg and Moore noted in their *Theoretical Perspectives on Human Rights*:

> The proliferation of literary and cultural texts telling the stories of past and current human rights violations clearly necessitates an understanding of human rights philosophies and frameworks; less obvious, perhaps, is the extent to which the critical insights gained through literary readings in the past fifty years might be brought to bear in human rights contexts – in the field and in legal, activist, and scholarly sites – to open the foundations of shared rights norms to new interpretations (Swanson Goldberg, Schultheis Moore 2012, p. 1).

This will be my critical focus, as I examine contemporary Indigenous Australian literature. Beforehand, however, I would like to say a few words on the close and yet not unequivocal ties that bind human rights and social justice, and how emotions stirred by the aesthetics and ethics of literature can relate to this nexus.

The Universal Declaration of Human Rights (UDHR) was endorsed in 1948, a landmark moment for a broad range of discourses on international law and the practice of human rights in the twentieth century. As Goldberg and Moore point out, the UDHR originated from the imperialistic perspective embedded in the nationalistic and proto-globalized balance of power at the end of WW2. This means that we have to be aware that "the theoretical implications of interdisciplinary work in human rights and literature are posed within this aura of contestation, critique, and deep desire for social justice" (Swanson Goldberg, Schultheis Moore 2012, p. 1).

Nevertheless, the UDHR perspective has been influential ever since and continues to inform viable approaches striving for the protection and preservation of social justice:

> Whether or not the language of human "rights", with its nationalist and juridical parameters and moral idealism, is the most efficacious and ethical framework for the work of securing dignity for all peoples remains in question. [...] Generalizing from the scene of torture to preventable human suffering of both acute and chronic kinds, we must understand the role to be played by human rights, with its instrumentalization in international law and politics, in ending suffering and striving for human dignity and justice – even as we recognize its imperialist origins and complicities with global power and corruption (Swanson Goldberg, Schultheis Moore 2012, p. 3).

Elizabeth Anker notes some consequences of this complex legacy:

> The global culture of human rights has, among countless advances, worked to combat the oppression of women, to consolidate international opposition to torture, genocide, and severe rights infringements, to minimize conditions of economic disenfranchisement, and to encourage sociopolitical rapprochement in the aftermath of rights abuses.

And again:

> It is hard to imagine a viable approach to social justice today that does not rely on the language of human rights. The proliferation of the many norms and ideals associated with human rights no doubt represents a hallmark achievement in international law, at the same time as it exemplifies the salutary repercussions of globalization. The late twentieth and twenty-first centuries have, in turn, come to be widely touted as the era of human rights – a sentiment that captures both the growing preponderance of rights talk and the immense promise that it invariably carries. This internationalization of human rights has led Michael Ignatieff to deem human rights "the lingua franca of global moral thought" and Elie Wiesel to call them a "world-wide secular religion" (Anker 2012, p. 1).

Let us now return to the connection between human rights and literature, one that, grounded on the ideal line of continuity between human rights and social justice, has its roots in the distant past. I would say it dates back at least to classical καλοκἀγαθία. This ancient insistence on the ethical quality of aesthetics also raised another fundamental question concerning the role of emotions in the pursuit of social justice via artistic expression. Of course, this finds its counterpoint in the alleged emotional detachment of those who perpetrate crimes against humanity, at least those who don't fall along the sadistic spectrum. As anticipated above, on this matter my focus dwells first on the Romantic period and recalls PB Shelley's reflections on the role of the poet in the human assemblage. The author of *The Necessity of Atheism* (1811) writes what follows in *A Defense of Poetry* (1821), somehow also echoing Weisel's and Ignatieff's position as noted in the previous quotation from Anker:

Every original language near to its source is in itself the chaos of a cyclic poem: the copiousness of lexicography and the distinctions of grammar are the works of a later age, and are merely the catalogue and the form of the creations of poetry. 3 But poets, or those who imagine and express this indestructible order, are not only the authors of language and of music, of the dance, and architecture, and statuary, and painting: *they are the institutors of laws, and the founders of civil society, and the inventors of the arts of life*, and the teachers, who draw into a certain propinquity with the beautiful and the true that partial apprehension of the agencies of the invisible world which is called religion. Hence all original religions are allegorical, or susceptible of allegory, and, like Janus, have a double face of false and true. Poets, according to the circumstances of the age and nation in which they appeared, were called, in the earlier epochs of the world, legislators, or prophets: a poet essentially comprises and unites both these characters. [...]

The tragedies of the Athenian poets are as mirrors in which the spectator beholds himself, under a thin disguise of circumstance, stripped of all but that ideal perfection and energy which everyone feels to be the internal type of all that he loves, admires, and would become. The *imagination is enlarged by a sympathy* with pains and passions so mighty, that they distend in their conception the capacity of that by which they are conceived; the good affections are strengthened by pity, indignation, terror, and sorrow "reason respects the differences, and imagination the similitudes of things (Shelley 1821, pp. 3–8).[1]

And this has to do with "Sympathy", in the etymological sense of the word, as "to feel with".

A line of continuity that goes back to Romantic aesthetics is to be found in Martha Nussbaum's work on the ethics and aesthetics of emotion. Nussbaum's perspective leads us back to the importance of stories: "emotions, unlike many of our beliefs, are not taught to us directly through propositional claims about the world, either abstract or concrete. They are taught, above all, through stories" (Nussbaum 1998, 226). Here the focus on the subjective quality of emotion returns: "Emotions contain an ineliminable reference to me, to the fact that it is my scheme of goals and projects. They see the world from my point of view" (Nussbaum 2001, 52). Most remarkable, however, in Nussbaum's philosophical position, especially as expounded in *Poetic Justice* (1995), is the idea that the emotions aroused by stories influence behavior, *i.e.*, that they have ethical value and consequences. Emotion is seen as a source of knowledge and relation, and this overturns the well-established Western tradition prejudice that considers emotion to be detrimental to both judgment and moral behavior (Locatelli 2017, p. 77). Emotions are thus freed from the grey area of mere impulsiveness, and become repositories of definitive cognitive, relational, and ethical power.

---

1 Emphasis mine.

Literature then – and this leads us to one of my central points – is a great catalyst for social and political justice: it sharpens our sensitivity to the world of the other, in a way that is neither prejudicial nor casual. In fact, it articulates an emotional response for the reader that is also defined in ethical terms, setting parameters that require identification with the other, alongside differentiation and autonomy. Emotional responses to narratives both promote and cultivate the dynamics of an empathic response, as opposed to what happens with the "economic mind", which is blind "to the fact that human life is something mysterious and not altogether fathomable" (Nussbaum 2001, 433). This empathic response also nurtures the sense of an ethical response, promoting the "poetic justice" that emerges from the interaction between "literary imagination and public life" and which also affects social justice.

Human Rights and their Discontents

It is a fact that colonial and postcolonial contexts (and their social justice) are inevitably linked to the question of rights, which in turn are inevitably implicated when one is confronted by strategies of aggression (this is one of their controversial aspects, after all; the discourse on rights is usually raised when they come up short, as exemplified by the 1948 UDHR, which followed one of the most tragic pages in the history of humanity). In his *History of Queensland*, historian Raymond Evans points to the brevity of colonial history compared to all that had come before. Yet, the nearly two hundred years of the Australian state colonial history occupies the most space in his reflections:

> Dinosaurs persisted for around 75 million years, dying out inexplicably some 65 million years ago. Aeons later, humankind arrived probably 50 000-60 000 years ago – and began a steady colonization of the continent across the next 10000 years. By contrast, British, European and Asian colonists came only during the last 180 years. A truly proportional telling of even the human story of this place would grant them only a small concluding paragraph (Evans 2007, pp. 1–2).

This same thought is expressed in Judith Wright's verses, summarized in the inspired and condensed tones of poetic language:

> The blue crane fishing in Cooloolah's twilight
> has fished there longer than our centuries.

On the one hand, in colonial and postcolonial contexts, human rights have been articulated in an institutionalized and essentially Eurocentric way that risks becoming a form of instrumentalization for other interests, that may conflict with cultural traditions based on assumptions that deviate conspicuously from that worldview, as Slavoj Zizek argues in his provocative "Against Human

Rights", "what the 'human rights of Third World suffering victims' effectively means today, in the predominant discourse, is the right of Western powers themselves to intervene politically, economically, culturally and militarily in the Third World countries of their choice, in the name of defending human rights" (Zizek 2005, p. 28). The use of the expression Third World would perhaps benefit from some further specification, and anyway it doesn't apply to every colonial and postcolonial context, but the message, with reference to what has been said above, is clear.

On the other hand, in colonial and postcolonial contexts, human rights may be construed in different or context-specific ways. For example, they often intersect and overlap with other fundamental issues, such as land rights. This is certainly the case in Australia, which at the very beginning of colonial exploitation denied the fundamental rights of First Nations to be "free and equal in dignity and rights" and to "life, liberty and the security of person" with the preposterous principle of *terra nullius*. This was based on the specious idea that Australia was a *terra nullius*, a formula that denies not so much the existence of the Indigenous peoples, as the existence of *a relationship of legal right* between them and the land, thus overlooking and consequently breaking the ancestral pact which was also the root of a whole system of living. The first denial of the human rights of the Indigenous peoples of Australia, then, lies precisely in this, in the negation of their right to land, and this is a situation that over the decades has been thematized, represented, denounced, and brought to public attention precisely by literary texts, which have thereby helped to elaborate a political position and also a vocabulary for the vindication of such rights.

Indigenous Literature and Human Rights

This leads us back to the quote in the title of my paper: "Right us a wrong and break the thrall / That keeps us low". These lines come from a poem by Oodgeroo Noonuccal, *An Appeal*, where we also read: "Must we native Old Australians / In our own land rank as aliens?". *An Appeal* was published in 1964 in the poetic collection *We Are Going* (Oodgeroo 1964), that finally brought the Aboriginal question to the forefront of debate in Australia. Up until that moment, this question had been silenced by colonial rule and postcolonial neglect; these lines were written only three years before the referendum which finally, after nearly two centuries of British rule, changed the Constitution so that, Aboriginal and Torres Strait Islander peoples would be finally counted as part of the official population, and the Commonwealth would be able to make laws for them like for all other Australians. The investiture of writers as fighters for social justice is also clearly foregrounded in the text of the poem:

> Writers, who have the nation's ear,
> Your pen is a sword opponents fear,
> Speak of our evils loud and clear
> That all may know.

After all, *We Are Going* is a paradigmatic case of how literature can act as a political force. It was through this collection of poetry that issues that are still prominent today in the country's slow process of Reconciliation began to become part of a shared heritage. The collection opens with a poem that is titled *Aboriginal Charter of Rights*, which weaves into its poetic discourse a series of vindications of rights that fit right into the framework of the UDHR:

> Give us welcome, not aversion,
> Give us choice, not cold coercion,
> Status, not discrimination,
> Human rights, not segregation.
> You the law, like Roman Pontius,
> Make us proud, not colour-conscious;
> Give the deal you still deny us,
> Give goodwill, not bigot bias;
> Give ambition, not prevention,
> Confidence, not condescension;
> Give incentive, not restriction,
> Give us Christ, not crucifixion.

Poetic language names and highlights specific issues related to the law and human rights: freedom and equality without distinctions based on race, colour, sex, language, religion; preventing situations that involve slavery or servitude, cruelty, inhuman or degrading treatment. And there is also a reference to a "deal", that leads us to an outstanding issue at the core of Australian decolonization up to the present time: the need for a Treaty with Indigenous people, as Australia is the only country in the Commonwealth that still lacks one. In fact, Indigenous literature has always played a vital role in the vindication of First Nations rights and has helped to pinpoint and express the "dispossessed" perspective of the colonized, shaping renewed awareness of the state of social justice in the country, or the justice to which the country should aspire (Di Blasio 2019). Often these instances are consolidated precisely around the issue of land, in the context of the special consideration and representation of physical spaces. This is a real *locus criticus* in contemporary Australia, which is still engaged in the search for a *Makarrata*, the Yolngu word for a shared treaty that would improve the legal representation of Indigenous Australians and enshrine their right to land.[2] The

---

[2] Among the most recent political and cultural initiatives in this sense it is worth mentioning the Uluru Statement from the Heart: https://ulurustatement.org/.

physical space of the land, experienced from the historical perspectives of Indigenous people and whites, has special ethical and emotional bearing, affecting its representation in literature, both politically and subjectively.

Kim Scott, in his novels in which history and fiction are 'blended' and integrated, also continually alludes to and thematizes the issue of rights in respect to land, place, and space. *Taboo* (Scott 2017), the last novel in a trilogy that includes *Benang: From the Heart* (1999) and *That Deadman Dance* (2010), notably rethinks (and decolonizes) contemporary Australian history, going beyond a mere critical gaze to offer a true rewriting of history and identity. If the frontier wars of the early nineteenth-century colonial era find expression in *That Deadman Dance*, and the assimilationist policies of the Twentieth century are thematized in *Benang*, Reconciliation, *i.e.*, the official political process that inaugurates the participatory turn in white-indigenous relations in the new century and millennium, is the 'institutional' theme of *Taboo*.

Let's observe how the centrality of land rights as constitutive of a subjective and collective identity emerges in the following segments from *Benang* and *Taboo*.

The first quote is taken from *Benang*:

> "Sing? Perhaps that is not the right word, because it is not really singing. And it is not really me who sings, for although I touch the earth only once in my performance – leaving a single footprint in white sand and ash – through me we hear the rhythm of many feet pounding the earth, and the strong pulse of countless hearts beating. Together, we listen to the creak and rustle of various plants in various winds, the countless beatings of different wings, the many strange and musical calls of animals who have come from this place right here. And, deep in the chill night, ending the song, the curlew's cry. Death bird, my people say. Obviously, however, I am alive. Am bringing life. People smile at me, say: 'You can always tell.' 'You can't hide who you are.' 'You feel it, here?' And, tapping their fists on my chest, 'Speak it from the heart'" (Scott 1999, p. 15).

This passage is characterized by a poignant consideration of physical and natural space in the reconstitution of the identity of the individual and the community. There is an intrinsic, earthly physicality in acknowledging oneself as a subject, and this recognition concurrently tends toward an authenticity of emotional feeling and the regeneration of a social ecology. It is worth noticing that this same physicality of space and place in ethical and emotional relationship to the self resonates in one of the most recent petitions by Australian Aboriginal leaders, the Uluru Statement from the Heart, presented in 2017 to change the constitution of Australia and "seek a Makarrata Commission to supervise a process of agreement-making between governments and First Nations and truth-telling about our history".[3]

---

[3] Uluru Statement from the Heart, https://ulurustatement.org/the-statement/view-the-statement/.

Taboo, a novel deeply connected to the land, includes a narrative scene about just such cultural confrontation with a difficult past, rooted in the management, involvement, and divergent consideration of the physicality of places.[4] The collective, and even official, event of the opening of a "Peace Park" at the site of a massacre of Indigenous people in the 1800s embodies and symbolizes this theme well. Indeed, the public occasion that coalesces around individual memories experienced from divergent positions functions as a powerful tool for creating an ethical awareness of cultural memory itself, also centered on the denial and recognition of rights. On the occasion of the opening of the park, and over the course of the narrative, White and Indigenous characters from different as well as intersecting individual and collective histories visit that 'incriminated' land together, marked by a trauma that seems indelible. Together they break a taboo and engage in a journey of discovery of new forms of coexistence, not only cohabitation. The breaking of the taboo, in particular, is condensed into the collective acknowledgement of the site of the massacre, the site of the denial of the right to life, security, and land. The earth is mother in the Indigenous *Weltanschauung*; its elements metonymically evoke her creative force; the bones that remain after the massacre, a sign of the violence of colonization, are a watershed not only between a before and an after but between the ancestral right to happiness, land, and life, and its absence, as hinted at in the following passage leading us to conclusion:

> They'd all be kept busy; a range of activities had been planned, Ruby said, trying out some things we'll do later, led by some of our community people, and we'll develop a program for camps for school kids, and for rehab and other groups. Culture and Community Development, she said, the capital letters loud in her voice. She repeated this phrase many times, along with Funding and Program of Activities. Plus, a lot of the mob just need to Keep Busy. One day, she said, we'll have workshops on art, making artefacts, story and song. Try some of those things ourselves, then tomorrow, or maybe the day after, she said – like promising dessert after you'd eaten your vegetables – we'll be visiting some Significant Sites.
> This was a Special Occasion, she finally said. Main reason we're here is the opening of the Peace Park. It'd be deadly to do a presentation, you know, she said once again, a Cultural Presentation, Reconciliation, someone said. Acknowledgement.
> 'Milton, you'll speak, won't you?' Milton nodded noncommittally. 'Wilfred?'
> 'Mmm.'
> 'We've planned some lovely walks. Some of the boys slashed paths. Lovely walks. Our old people used to walk everywhere. No diabetes, no heart disease, no mental health issues with them.'
> 'But, we can't do all that.'
> 'Were planning for the future. Culture and Community Development,' and again she said, more emphatically, 'Acknowledgement. Reconciliation.'

---

4 A previous work which deals with *Taboo* and the emotional implications of the physicality of places and objects in a neurocognitive perspective is Di Blasio 2021.

They moved away, coalescing in little groups. Ruby and Kathy, with Wally a less enthusiastic recruit, shepherded them from place to place.

Colonialism is a story of rights denied, and post-colonialism a painful journey of reconstitution. Literature has contributed and contributes significantly to this regeneration. To decolonize, after all, is to rewrite, in the ways of law as in the ways of art, a history of social justice.

Works Cited

Anker, Elizabeth S.: *Fictions of Dignity: Embodying Human Rights in World Literature.* Cornell University Press, Ithaca 2012.
Carr Vellino, Brenda: 'Everything I Know about Human Rights I Learned from Literature: Human Rights Literacy in the Canadian Literature Classroom', in Sugars, C. (ed.): *Postcolonialism, Pedagogy, and Canadian Literature.* University of Ottawa Press, Ottawa 2004, pp. 135–150.
Di Blasio, Francesca: 'Affective Narratology, Cultural Memory, and Aboriginal Culture in Kim Scott's Taboo', in Vernay J-F. (ed.): *The Rise of the Australian Neurohumanities.* Routledge, Abigdon / New York 2021, pp. 40–65.
Di Blasio, Francesca: '*We Are Going* by Oodgeroo Noonuccal. Aboriginal Epos, Australian History, Universal Poetry', in: Le Simplegadi, 2019/17, pp. 119–127.
Evans, Raymond: *A History of Queensland.* Cambridge University Press, Cambridge, New York / Melbourne 2007.
Locatelli, Angela: 'Emotions and/in Religion Reading Sigmund Freud, Rudolph Otto, and William James', in: Jandl, I. / Knaller, S. / Schönfellner, S. / Tockner, G. (eds.): *Writing Emotions: Theoretical Concepts and Selected Case Studies in Literature.* Transcript Verlag, Bielefeld 2017, pp. 77–96.
Locatelli, Angela: *La conoscenza della Letteratura/The Knowledge of Literature* Vol. I. Sestante, Bergamo 2002.
Oodgeroo Noonuccal: *We Are Going.* Jacaranda Press, Brisbane 1964.
Scott, Kim: *Benang: From the Heart.* Fremantle Arts Centre Press, North Fremantle 1999.
Scott, Kim: *Taboo.* Picador Australia, Sydney 2017.
Scott, Kim: *That Deadman Dance*, Picador Australia, Sydney 2010.
Swanson Goldberg, Elizabeth / Schultheis Moore, Alexandra: *Theoretical Perspectives on Human Rights.* Routledge, New York 2012.
Zizek, Slavoj: 'Against Human Rights', in: New Left Review 2005/34, pp. 115–31.

Web Sources

Shelley, Percy Bysshe: *A Defense of Poetry*, pp. 1–20, https://resources.saylor.org/wwwresources/archived/site/wp-content/uploads/2011/01/A-Defense-of-Poetry.pdf (Accessed November 2023).
Uluru Statement from the Heart, https://ulurustatement.org/ (accessed November 2023).

Luca Pinelli
(University of Bergamo & Université Sorbonne Nouvelle)

Of Monsters and Cannibals: Literature and the Body between Virginia Woolf's Essays and Simone de Beauvoir's Philosophy and Literary Theory

As many critics have emphasised in the last few decades, one of the basic assumptions inherent in a liberal, humanist understanding of literature is the fact that it is the product of a purely mental activity. When it comes to reading and writing, the body is generally regarded to be a useless appendix, something that can easily be discarded or at least reduced to the role of a mediator of creative processes through sensorimotor functions. In opposition to this widely held belief, critics like António Damásio (1994) and Peter Brooks (1993) famously argued that philosophy and literature have in fact been concerned with the body since ancient times, with Descartes' positing of the mind/body dualism resulting in an often costly error. More recently, Thomas Fuchs (2017) has drawn attention to the perils of understanding the brain as the ultimate terrain where humanity resides, a terrain which the neurosciences are tasked with exploring and investigating, thereby reducing the notion of human subjectivity to one – oftentimes, for practical purposes isolated – organ.

Before the recent critical reappraisal of the mind/body dualism, both Virginia Woolf and Simone de Beauvoir lamented the neglect to which the body had been subjected in literature and philosophy. In her 1930 essay *On Being Ill*, Virginia Woolf famously stated that

> with a few exceptions […] literature does its best to maintain that its concern is with the mind; that the body is a sheet of plain glass through which the soul looks straight and clear, and, save for one or two passions such as desire and greed, is dull, and negligible and non-existent. On the contrary, the very opposite is true. All day, all night the body intervenes; blunts or sharpens, colours or discolours, turns to wax in the warmth of June, hardens to tallow in the murk of February (Woolf 2009, p. 195).[1]

---

1 While an earlier version of the essay appeared in the *New Criterion* in January 1926, I prefer to cite the later version published by The Hogarth Press in volume form because it integrates some slight edits which, as will be argued below, are more in line with Woolf's (and Beauvoir's) thought.

In a similar vein, Beauvoir bemoans the treatment reserved to the body in philosophy in her second philosophical essay, *The Ethics of Ambiguity* (1947):

> As long as there have been men and they have lived, they have all felt this tragic ambiguity of their condition, but as long as there have been philosophers and they have thought, most of them have tried to mask it. They have striven to reduce mind to matter, or to reabsorb matter into mind, or to merge them within a single substance. Those who have accepted the dualism have established a hierarchy between body and soul which permits of considering as negligible the part of the self which cannot be saved (Beauvoir 2018, p. 6).

Although their educational background was clearly different,[2] as evidenced even in such short passages as these, Woolf and Beauvoir come to articulate similar concerns over the traditional understanding of the mind/body dichotomy. Beauvoir distances herself from all forms of reductionism, whether idealist or materialist, because being human for her means being tragically and inevitably ambiguous, torn as we are between operating as consciousnesses in the world and experiencing ourselves as objects of other people's actions, bound to the materiality of the world; she is equally wary, however, of a philosopher like Descartes, who, despite acknowledging this profound ambiguity inherent in humankind, decides to construct a hierarchy between body and mind, one where, as registered by Damásio, the rational mind comes to embody subjectivity at the expense of body and emotion. As we will see, Woolf similarly draws attention to the centrality of the body in the act of reading and in that of writing, as well as in our lives more broadly. This contribution intends to shed light on how Woolf's essays and Beauvoir's philosophy and literary theory, if brought together, can reflect their authors' interpretation of literature as the privileged site of intercorporeality, a concept derived from phenomenology which insists on a relational, corporeal understanding of the self. For Woolf and Beauvoir, then, it is especially through the reading and writing process, as we will see, that human beings are constituted as intercorporeal subjects.

One last question needs to be addressed before we can move on to the first section, however. To re-adapt the opening sentence of *A Room of One's Own*, "But, you may say, we asked you to speak about [literature and the body] – what has that got to do with [monsters and cannibals]? I will try to explain" (Woolf 2015, p. 3).[3] The two sections that follow take Woolf's somewhat provocative

---

2 While Woolf never received a formal education at university – except for a few courses at the King's College London Ladies' Department –, Beauvoir studied philosophy and passed the prestigious *agrégation* exam in philosophy at the young age of 21, coming second only to Sartre. For Woolf, cf. Snaith 2021; for Beauvoir, cf. Kirkpatrick 2019.

3 As is known, the original opening passage of *A Room of One's Own* reads: "But, you may say, we asked you to speak about women and fiction, what has that got to do with a room of one's own? I will try to explain".

definition of the body as a monster and that of the novel as a cannibal as the hinges on which the argument will turn. It will be argued that Woolf and Beauvoir take, on the one hand, the body to be a monstrous construction and, on the other, literature to provide readers and writers alike with the instruments to expand their own bodies beyond their physical boundaries.

"This monster, the body": The Living Body between Woolf and Beauvoir

After opening *On Being Ill* with the polemical statement about how the body participates in the supposedly mental processes of reading and writing, Woolf emphasises how the body and the soul/mind are in fact not only irreducible to each other – as Beauvoir points out – but they cannot be extricated from one another.

> The creature within can only gaze through the pane – smudged or rosy; it cannot separate off from the body like the sheath of a knife or the pod of a pea for a single instant; it must go through the whole unending procession of changes, heat and cold, comfort and discomfort, hunger and satisfaction, health and illness, until there comes the inevitable catastrophe; the body smashes itself to smithereens, and the soul (it is said) escapes (Woolf 2009, p. 195).[4]

Although the Western tradition has tended to think of literature as the product of intellect and soul, reading and writing are actually material activities which are inevitably affected by the position and the state of our bodies: as circumstances change, so do our bodies and, as a result, the literature they produce or absorb – so much so that, as Woolf will argue in the second part of the essay, being ill results in being 'rash' even in our reading or writing, a state that was insightfully summarised by Sarah Pett as "both a sense of detachment, even liberation, from social norms and an unmediated, profoundly phenomenological engagement with the world and its inhabitants" (Pett 2019, p. 33). The "creature within" which in a previous essay, "Montaigne" (1925), was shown to be an elusive shape-shifter that writers have to represent in its vitality and in all its protean manifestations without ever crystallising it in one definitive form,[5] is described here as though it

---

4 I have chosen to use the last version of the text Woolf prepared for publication, namely the 1930 volume *On Being Ill*, rather than the earlier text. Only minor alterations were made to the 1926 text, but it is clear that the last published version is more in line with Woolf's philosophy than the earlier version, as will be argued below.

5 "The phantom is through the mind and out the window before we can lay salt on its tail, or slowly sinking and returning to the profound darkness which it has lit up momentarily with a wandering light"; "Really she is the strangest creature in the world, […] – in short, so complex, so indefinite, corresponding so little to the version which does duty for her in public, that a

were encased in a glass cage, the body: this transparent material can in fact be affected by changes in temperature or situation and thus our own view of it may be obfuscated or simply altered by the very fact that the intellect is always embodied. Unlike "the sheath of a knife or the pod of a pea", the body is one with the intellect, so that when the former experiences a specific situation or feeling, the latter is also affected by it. What we tend to think of as a perennially transparent glass cage which does not have a direct impact on what it contains is described by Woolf here as a material which actively shapes its contents: body and mind are irreducible and unassimilable to one another, their constitutive differences preventing them quite paradoxically from being separated. When the body "smashes itself to smithereens" as a result of "the inevitable catastrophe" that is death, the soul is said to escape, Woolf's brackets suggesting here a position of epistemic humility which reports – rather than prescribes – a commonsensical or religious view.

As she goes on to argue:

> But of all this daily drama of the body there is no record. People write always about the doings of the mind; the thoughts that come to it; its noble plans; how it has civilised the universe. They show it ignoring the body in the philosopher's turret; or kicking the body, like an old leather football, across leagues of snow and desert in the pursuit of conquest or discovery. Those great wars which the body wages with the mind a slave to it, in the solitude of the bedroom against the assault of fever or the oncome of melancholia, are neglected. Nor is the reason far to seek. To look these things squarely in the face would need the courage of a lion tamer; a robust philosophy; a reason rooted in the bowels of the earth. Short of these, this monster, the body, this miracle, its pain, will soon make us taper into mysticism, or rise, with rapid beats of the wings, into the raptures of transcendentalism (Woolf 2009, p. 195 f.).

Woolf draws attention here to how philosophers ignore the body in their "turrets", the latter space clearly recalling the lofty, abstract ideals of thinking as opposed to the grounded materiality of the body. In the same sentence, she then emphasises how bodies are mobilised for war and discovery, before suggesting that there are other perhaps more internal or intimate battles that the body "wages with the mind a slave to it", not out on the battlefield but rather "in the solitude of the bedroom". While a philosopher's turret may be described as an elevated space dedicated to reflection, which on some level recalls Montaigne's famous refuge, this bedroom creates an intimate atmosphere where a war against illness can rage on undiscussed by literature and philosophy – a room which in its

---

man might spend his life merely in trying to run her to earth" (Woolf 1994, p. 72 f.). On the monstrosity of the essay form in Montaigne and Woolf cf. Karshan 2020; cf. Bugliani 2018 for a closer look at the essay in the English tradition as well as for the meta-reflexive quality of the genre which Woolf inherited from Montaigne.

very name contains a place for horizontal rest, the bed, as opposed to the vertical thinking embodied by the turret.

The reason for this neglect is to be found, as she argues, in the fact that what is needed in order to address our corporeality is not only "the courage of a lion tamer", as the beast that is our body both in its materiality and as a subject matter must be mastered, but also "a robust philosophy" and "a reason rooted in the bowels of the earth" rather than, as is implied, in the 'turret' of the body, namely our heads. Underneath the textual surface, Woolf is already suggesting that there exists a profound gap between the horizontal rest required by the body's suppleness and susceptibility and the supposed vertical mobility – both physical and mental – that the mind is generally regarded to represent.

Interestingly, in her final revision of the 1926 text, Woolf slightly altered one of these sentences: while in the first version she had written "Those great wars which it [i.e. the body] wages *by itself*, with the mind a slave to it" (Woolf 1994, p. 318),[6] here she chose to redact "by itself" and made the subject explicit: "Those great wars which the body wages with the mind a slave to it" (Woolf 2009, p. 196). This slight change clearly signals how Woolf does not intend to imply that the body, like the mind, can be conceived of as a solipsistic construct, namely as an entity existing in a vacuum, in isolation from the world: there are no wars that the body fights 'by itself', as there is always something it is responding to that is paradoxically both external and internal. This slight edit by Woolf already points to the fact that the body is not an object commanded by reason but rather represents the embodied, relational subject every human being is despite all (patriarchal, liberal, humanist) efforts to claim otherwise.

In contrast to the widespread idea that the body is an object that is substantially different from the intellect, where subjectivity is generally claimed to reside, phenomenologists like Maurice Merleau-Ponty emphasised how humanity cannot be reduced to the status of species but must be inscribed within history: as he argues in *The Phenomenology of Perception* (1945), "Man is a historical idea and not a natural species"; as a result, "All that we are, we are on the basis of a *de facto* situation which we appropriate to ourselves and which we ceaselessly transform by a sort of *escape* which is never an unconditioned freedom" (Merleau-Ponty 2002, p. 198).[7] This passage is echoed by Beauvoir in the Biology chapter of *The Second Sex* (1949), where, after exploring specific biological data regarding human and nonhuman animals, she argues that

> Only within a human perspective can the female and the male be compared in the human species. But the definition of man is that he is a being who is not given, who

---

6 Emphasis added.
7 Emphasis in the original. For an exploration of the similarities and differences between Merleau-Ponty and Beauvoir in relation to phenomenology, cf. Heinämaa 2003, Ehrsam 2020.

makes himself what he is. As Merleau-Ponty rightly said, man is not a natural species: he is an historical idea. Woman is not a fixed reality but a becoming; she has to be compared with man in her becoming, that is, her *possibilities* have to be defined: what skews the issues so much is that she is being reduced to what she was, to what she is today, while the question concerns her capacities; the fact is that her capacities manifest themselves clearly only when they have been realised: but the fact is also that when one considers a being who is transcendence and surpassing, it is never possible to close the books (Beauvoir 2011, p. 46).[8]

Just because women were prevented from accessing certain professions or positions, this does not mean that they are incapable of carrying out some intellectual or complex tasks, Beauvoir argues: within an understanding of subjectivity as becoming, it makes no sense to think that what was and what is would have to remain the same in the future. The biological reductionism that is typical of patriarchal ideology, one whereby women are nothing but their sex and their body, is here censured by Beauvoir by appealing to the freedom and the material becoming inherent in every human being: what women are capable of cannot be considered without taking into account the material conditions impinging upon their agency.

The monstrosity of the human body, for Beauvoir, derives from the fact that it is what she terms a *situation*. As she explains, "in the position I adopt – that of Heidegger, Sartre and Merleau-Ponty – [...] if the body is not a *thing*, it is a situation: it is our grasp on the world and the outline for our projects" (Beauvoir 2011, p. 46). Because woman as a subject is not a fixed essence but an historical becoming, her body must be interpreted as a situation, not simply as being *in* situation. As Toril Moi aptly pointed out in "What Is a Woman?" (1999), what many commentators misunderstood about Beauvoir's philosophy in the following decades is precisely this subtle distinction between being *a situation* and being *in a situation*, the latter being a more familiar idea to anyone exhibiting a sociological understanding of phenomena. "For Beauvoir", Moi remarks, "these are different claims, equally important and equally true, but not reducible to one another": "My situation is not *outside* me, it does not relate to me as an object to a subject; it is a synthesis of facticity and freedom. [...] We are always in a situation, but the situation is always part of us" (Moi 1999, p. 59, 65). Because subjectivity is embodied, the body too is ambiguous: the biological data which are normally

---

8 It ought to be noted that the first English translation of *Le Deuxième Sexe*, penned by zoologist H. M. Parshley in 1953, was extremely flawed in that it excised around 10–15% of the original and was a poor representation of Beauvoir's philosophical sophistication; the retranslation by Borde and Malovany-Chevallier has fared much better in recent scholarship, though of course it has not made it unscathed either. I have chosen to use their translation because it strikes me as a good version of the original, but to get a better sense of the vicissitudes of the text in English cf. Mann / Ferrari 2017 and Bogic 2009–2010.

used to reduce women to their bodies are shown by Beauvoir to be insufficient to explain how and why woman has been cast as Other in patriarchal ideology; as a result, different sorts of documents – historical, philosophical, anthropological, sociological, even literary – ought to be mobilised in order to understand this ambiguous amalgamation of nature and culture – or "natureculture", to borrow Donna Haraway's famous coinage[9] – that is a subject, and more specifically one that through femininity has been made subservient to men and patriarchy. While saying that we are always situated means operating a *sociology* of the world, relying on the idea that the body is a situation produces a *phenomenology* of the world, arguably even an existentialist one – an intuition which has had far-reaching repercussions on the feminist thought of Donna Haraway and Sandra Harding among others.[10]

At any rate, as Moi stresses, "Anyone who tries to read *The Second Sex* through the lens of the sex/gender distinction is bound to misunderstand Beauvoir" (Moi 1999, p. 73): what had by the 1970s become a Beauvoirian dictum, namely "One is not born, but rather becomes, [a] woman" (Beauvoir 2011, p. 293),[11] does not anticipate the notion of gender, unlike what Judith Butler argued in her commentary on (Parshley's truncated, unphilosophical version of) *The Second Sex*.[12] In Beauvoir's phenomenological interpretation of the body, the latter cannot be reduced to a set of biological data – what we would now call 'sex' – precisely because, like Merleau-Ponty, she opposes the idea that human beings are nothing but a natural species that can be studied by science. In contrast to this notion of the body as an object, both Merleau-Ponty and Beauvoir propose the notion of the body as a situation made up of both facticity (biological data) and freedom (agency), to the effect that, as Moi encapsulated it, "The body is a historical sedimentation of our way of living in the world, and of the world's way of living with us" (Butler 1986 and 1999, p. 68). Not only is the body "our perspective on the world", it is also "engaged in a dialectical interaction with its surroundings, that is to say with all the other situations in which the body is placed" (Butler 1986 and 1999, p. 68), to such an extent that the subject/object dichotomy, the nature/culture divide, and the mind/body dualism are no longer tenable. From Beauvoir's perspective, differentiating between sex – the body and its biological data – and gender – the way we construct our identity according to pre-established categories – results in excluding the body from feminist theory, as happened

---

9 Cf. Haraway 2003.
10 Cf. Haraway 1988 and Harding 1992.
11 Borde and Malovany-Chevallier's translation strikingly redacted the indeterminate article 'a' from the sentence, a decision which understandably sparked some controversy among Beauvoir scholars: cf. Mann / Ferrari 2017.
12 Cf. Butler 1986 and 1999.

from the 1960s through to the 1990s according to Moi and as our present situation would confirm according to other contemporary feminists.[13]

As Sara Heinämaa showed, French phenomenologists like Beauvoir and Merleau-Ponty recovered the Husserlian distinction between the body-object (*Körper*) and the living body (*Leib*): in the former case, we relate to bodies as to "mere physical things", namely as to "pieces of inert matter, stone, or metal", whereas vegetable, animal, and human bodies fall in the latter category (Heinämaa 2002, p. 26). What really distinguishes the two terms, for Husserl as for Merleau-Ponty and Beauvoir, is our own attitude (*Einstellung*) to the body. In the case of the body-object, we experience the body as a "natural scientist" would, namely we "abstract all meaning, value, and purpose away from the bodies that we study" in order to "try to explain and predict their behaviour by subsuming them under some general laws"; in the second case, we experience living bodies "as meaningful and purposeful agents", as "*persons*", and "our own activity and interest is not in explaining or predicting the behaviour of others, but in responding to their movements and gestures" (Heinämaa 2002, p. 26). Thus, the naturalistic attitude insists on the physical, inert qualities of the body-object, while the personalistic attitude considers the body and the soul to be so intimately and inextricably connected that, precisely as Woolf suggested in *On Being Ill*, the soul "cannot separate off from the body like the sheath of a knife or the pod of a pea for a single instant" (Woolf 2009, p. 195). As Heinämaa aptly summarises Husserl's view, "The soul binds bodily functions and parts together into a spiritual unity that cannot be broken up or divided into autonomous parts. Thus, the organs and movements of our bodies form a similar stylistic unity as chapters, paragraphs, and sentences of a book" (Heinämaa 2002, p. 32).

From this phenomenological perspective, the body is not simply an object to be studied by scientists; rather, it is a materially entangled, intrinsically ambiguous situation which forms the basis and the limits for our own agency. As Ruth Groenhout summarises Beauvoir's philosophy of the body,

> Her account focuses on the lived social situations of people who exist as sexed beings in the midst of complex social structures, people whose bodies are always simultaneously

---

13 Besides Moi's prophetic intuition, cf. Federici 2020 and Froidevaux-Metterie 2021, who both emphasise how, despite being at the centre of most feminist struggles from the 1970s until now, the body has often been reduced to the inert matter of 'sex' in feminist theory, a matter which is and ought to be the object of study of science rather than the humanities. I acknowledge that Butler attempted to show how 'sex' itself is a discursive category, too, to the effect that "sex, by definition, [is] shown to have been gender all along" (Butler 1999, p. 12); however, I concur with Moi that this poststructuralist theorisation has often resulted in reducing the body to discourse and language, whereas Beauvoir's phenomenological understanding of intercorporeality still strikes me as an interesting, albeit often neglected, contribution to the topic.

biological, social, and imbued with value, and whose experiences respond to and shape the meaning of human existence (Groenhout 2017, p. 76).

This is precisely what Woolf may have had in mind when she suggested that reconnecting literature – or thinking broadly conceived – to the body requires a "reason rooted in the bowels of the earth" and, interestingly, a "robust philosophy" (Woolf 2009, p. 196). Through recourse to Beauvoir's feminist-phenomenological understanding of the body, it becomes clear how a change in our body leads to a change in our agency, in our interaction with other people and the world at large. Being bed-ridden, for instance, changes the perspective from which we observe and make the world: instead of participating in humanity's march for progress, we lie horizontal, or, as Woolf puts it, "we cease to be soldiers in the army of the upright; we become deserters" (Woolf 2009, p. 196). Being ill, for Woolf, means relinquishing the "illusion of a world so shaped that it echoes every groan, of human beings so tied together by common needs and fears that a twitch at one wrist jerks another" so that we are finally able to contemplate the sky "perhaps for the first time for years" and explore those "embryo lives which attend about us in early youth until 'I' suppressed them": as Woolf perfectly encapsulates it, "Left to ourselves we speculate thus carnally" (Woolf 2009, p. 200f.).

"That cannibal, the novel": Literature as Intercorporeality

What enables this carnal speculation is precisely literature, in Woolf's view: as she argues in *On Being Ill*, it is through poetry that we can finally imagine different lives and play different roles from that imposed by the 'I' that controls us. By relinquishing this first-person singular pronoun, human beings are finally able to connect to 'other' worlds and different existences, all of which are mediated through literature. As she points out in "A Letter to a Young Poet" (1932), literature – beyond generic distinctions – becomes obscure and difficult when one limits oneself to describing one's own position in the world; on the contrary, Woolf advises her reader, John Lehmann, to take part in a collective dance dictated by the sense of rhythm in the body: "All you need to do is to stand at the window and let your rhythmical sense open and shut, open, and shut, boldly and freely, until one thing melts in another, until the taxis are dancing with the daffodils, until a whole has been made from all these separate fragments", for "How can you learn to write if you write only about one single person?" (Woolf 2009, p. 315, 317). Reading, after all, Woolf argues, "is rather like opening the door to a horde of rebels who swarm out attacking one in twenty places at once", affecting different "senses" among which she interestingly names not only "the reason" and "the imagination", but also – and perhaps more crucially – "the eyes, the ears, the palms of the hands and the soles of the feet" (Woolf 2009, p. 315, 317). More than thirty years later, in 1964, Beauvoir was asked to give a lecture on the role of literature. During a debate organised by a communist magazine in Paris, she expressed her views of literature as "the privileged site of intersubjectivity" in these terms:

> The singularity of our situation is an irreducible fact. But at the same time there is a communication in this very separation. I mean that I am a subject who says "I," I am the only subject for myself who says "I," and it's the same thing for each one of you.
> Each person's life has a unique flavour that, in a sense, no one else can know. But it's the same thing for each of us.
> And I think that literature's good fortune is that it can surpass the other modes of communication and allow us to communicate in what separates us. Literature – if it is authentic – is a way of surpassing the separation by affirming it. It affirms the separation because when I read a book – a book that counts for me – someone is speaking to me; the author is part of his book. Literature only starts at that moment, the moment when I hear a singular voice (Beauvoir 2011b, p. 199f.).

Because reality for Beauvoir "is not a fixed being; it is a becoming", that is "a swirling of singular experiences that envelop each other while remaining separate" (Beauvoir 2011b, p. 200), literature becomes the only way we can paradoxically bridge the gap between our experience and other people's while at the same time reinforcing this separation, as our bodies become aware of their own relationality to the materiality of the world and of other people. Although the voice we can hear when we read an author's work is singular, it also open to the world and embraces all sorts of different experiences, so much so that, in one of her 1966 Japanese lectures, Beauvoir will stress that good novels have to be symphonic: the text and the author may be one in their appearance, but their existence, because it is a situation in a constant state of becoming, is to some extent plurally inflected (Beauvoir 2011b, p. 286).

This notion of singularity is of paramount importance: we are singular in both senses of the word, that is we are both individual and unique, and yet we all share this quality and in this sense we are already connected to one another, as Beauvoir remarks. Gillian Beer emphasised how this tension between singularity and plurality – what the critic terms "the communal" – animates Woolf's fiction, too, to the effect that "How to discover the communal in this singularity is the poet's and, her work suggests, should be the fiction writer's task" (Beer 1996, p. 60). Interestingly, one of the pieces of advice Woolf gives to the young poet is "Never think yourself singular, never think your own case much harder than other people's" (Woolf 2009, p. 308). It is clear that here she is using 'singular' in the sense of remarkable or unique, but at the same time if we keep this conversation with Beauvoir's essay in mind, we could take Woolf's term much further, seeing in the singular voice which for Beauvoir inaugurates literature as an embodied experience the Woolfian "body of the people" and "experience of the mass behind the single voice" (Woolf 2015, p. 49). In the same letter to Lehmann, Woolf points out how any young poet should feel part of a long tradition, one that guides him or her in his or her writing:

> Think of yourself rather as something much humbler and less spectacular, but to my mind, far more interesting – a poet in whom live all the poets of the past, from whom all poets in time to come will spring. You have a touch of Chaucer in you, and something of Shakespeare; Dryden, Pope, Tennyson – to mention only the respectable among your ancestors – stir in your blood and sometimes move your pen a little to the right or to the left. In short you are an immensely ancient, complex, and continuous character […] (Woolf 2015, p. 309).

This passage sheds light on how central time is in this view of literature: it is not just with our contemporaries that we share our existence, our situation, and our bodies, but also with our ancestors and predecessors. The intercorporeal quality of writing is here represented in the "touch" of different authors who "stir in your blood and sometimes move your pen a little to the right or to the left": if in *On Being Ill* Woolf theorised how literature and (inter)corporeality are far from being mutually exclusive aspects of humanity, here she is providing a material example of how this intercorporeal communication across spatial and temporal separation may happen. As she will summarise it in "The Leaning Tower" (1940), "Even the simplest story deals with more than one person, with more than one time" (Woolf 2011, p. 259).

In this sense, it could be argued that any human subject who reads is in fact, as Woolf suggests, "an immensely ancient, complex, and continuous character", too, one whose very existence depends on the sometimes tenuous connections with other human beings, past and present. In this spirit, *A Room of One's Own* famously closes with the future resurrection of Judith Shakespeare's body, an event that will only take place when women finally have access to money and rooms of their own:

> She [i. e. Judith Shakespeare] lives in you and me, and in many other women who are not here tonight, for they are washing up the dishes and putting the children to bed. But she lives; for great poets do not die; they are continuing presences; they need only the opportunity to walk among us in the flesh (Woolf 2011, p. 85f.).

These "continuing presences" are such because they have left us with some remains of their existences. They are not just spectral presences, they are not immaterial or evanescent; first and foremost, Woolf and Beauvoir seem to say in unison, they are embodied subjects whose works are stamped with their singular voices. To quote Woolf in the last version of "How Should One Read a Book?":

> Every literature, as it grows old, has its rubbish-heap, its record of vanished moments and forgotten lives told in faltering and feeble accents that have perished. But if you give yourself up to the delight of rubbish-reading you will be surprised, indeed you will be overcome, by the relics of human life that have been cast out to moulder (Woolf 2009, p. 577).

The reader's task is thus to collect these "relics of human life" from the past, absorb them, make them part of their own world through this "rubbish-reading". It is easy to see how this practice can be defined cannibalistic in a way: if literature offers us parts of other people's worlds and bodies, when we read we are in fact phagocytising them. Although Woolf referred to the novel as "the cannibal" because of its tendency to 'devour' other art forms (Woolf 1994, p. 435), this dialogue between the English author and Beauvoir has shown that this idea of cannibalism can be extended beyond the generic to include the literary *tout court*. Reading consists in bridging the gap that separates us from one another while reaffirming its existence; it implies the continuing presence of our predecessors, whose relics we go through and possibly take possession of; in annexing these 'other' worlds, we are also relinquishing our own sense of identity in favour of a more collective and embodied sense of our existence.

In opposition to the "elderly nekrophilist" Mr Peabody "and his like" (Woolf 1994, p. 307, 314) who are censured by Woolf in "A Letter to a Young Poet" for their decreeing the death of the art of letter-writing and of poetry, literature ought to be understood as a living, embodied relationship with other experiences across time and space, experiences which are clearly anchored to specific bodies with singular voices who are cannibalised in the intercorporeal act of writing as well as in the subsequent but equally intercorporeal act of reading. While Mr Peabody and the "large and highly respectable society of nekrophils" insist that "Keats is dead, Shelley is dead, Byron is dead" (Woolf 1994, p. 314), for Woolf these bodies are still living among us, they are Husserlian *Leiber*, Beauvoirian bodies in becoming ambiguously stamped with singularity and collectivity. As Gillian Beer perceptively remarked, "The deep values which she [i.e. Woolf] accords to communality is not a matter only of her sincerely learnt and practised socialism or her forcefully written (if not always practised) solidarity with other women"; rather, "It has to do with her practice of writing out of the mass and out the body".[14] It could be argued that the monstrosity of the body resides precisely in its appropriating other bodies, other experiences, other narratives; it is a monster whose confines are not clearly set but are in fact constantly expanding in all directions in the attempt to annex otherness and make it part of itself. Con-

---

14 Beer 1996, p. 50. As concerns Woolf's engagement with contemporary social movements, cf. Jones 2016, who retraces her involvement in activism and insightfully defines Woolf an ambivalent activist.

trary to our own perception of corporeality, our body does not simply end where we think it does: like a cannibal monster, it takes possession of the materiality around us, it phagocytises otherness and thus transforms our own constitution beyond the strictures imposed by a towering 'I'.

In "Professions for Women", Woolf famously said that in her professional life as a woman writer, she had to face two main challenges: one was "killing the Angel in the House", something she managed to do despite some initial difficulties dictated by her gender, and, two, "telling the truth about [her] own experiences as a body", which she thinks she did not solve, nor has any woman solved it yet (Woolf 2011, p. 483). This is because in her view there are still too many limitations imposed upon the so-called second sex, and although some progress has been made by 1931, when she gave the original speech to the London and National Society for Women's Service, or by 1933, when she revised the speech for publication, "this freedom is only a beginning; the room is your own, but it is still bare. It has to be furnished; it has to be decorated; it has to be shared" (Woolf 2011, p. 484). This notion of taking up space is fundamental to Woolf's idea of women's liberation: as is known, she argued in 1929 that women need a room of one's own so they can write and not be interrupted by constant demands for attention and care responsibilities; four years later, she seems to suggest that because women now have access to some professions, they have been given rooms, bare though they are. It is interesting to notice here that she does not simply suggest that these rooms have to be furnished and decorated, but she also states that this space has to be *shared*, perhaps because, as she wrote in "The Patron and the Crocus" (1925), "the crocus is an imperfect crocus until it has been shared" (Woolf 1994, p. 213). Literature as a method of communication serves precisely this purpose: it enables a writer to convey their own already plural, materially becoming, monstrously cannibalistic situation to somebody else and in doing so, it creates a continuity in time and space between different people, bodies, and worlds. In the spirit of sharing things, impressions, matter, we could say, literature may be regarded as a continuous ritualised trade of embodied experiences that never cease to exist in that they manage, through language, to transcend time and space, ensuring as it does that even the dead authors of the past continue to have a living, bodily relationship with the present.

In this context, reading does not simply amount to performing literary criticism; rather, it is a material becoming with the author, the text and the situation that are separated from us by time and space. As Woolf writes in the last version of "How Should One Read a Book?",

> Do not dictate to your author; try to become him. Be his fellow-worker and accomplice. If you hang back, and reserve and criticise at first, you are preventing yourself from getting the fullest possible value from what you read. But if you open your mind as

widely as possible, then signs and hints of almost imperceptible fineness, from the twist and turn of the first sentences, will bring you into the presence of a human being unlike any other. Steep yourself in this, acquaint yourself with this, and soon you will find that your author is giving you, or attempting to give you, something far more definite (Woolf 2009, p. 573f.).

That is, I would add, he or she is giving you access to his or her very material world, he or she is stimulating not just your mind, but your monstrous, shape-shifting body, a body that is constantly in the state of becoming, Beauvoir would suggest. Through this becoming other, we abandon our monolithic identity in favour of different embodied experiences that help us better understand the world we inhabit, the body we generally neglect, the past tradition that sustains us. In this embodied genealogy, in this state of becoming, our identity becomes monstrous and cannibalistic, perhaps, but it is only through this process that we can come to see literature as an intercorporeal act that overcomes separation and saves us from the despair of our own singularity. "Never think yourself singular," Woolf said to the young poet (Woolf 2009, p. 308); for you are always already plural, collective, protean when you read or write, we should add.

Works Cited

Beauvoir, Simone de: The Second Sex. Translated from the French by Constance Borde and Sheila Malovany-Chevallier. With an Introduction by Sheila Rowbotham. Picador, London 2011 [2009].

Beauvoir, Simone de: "The Useless Mouths" and Other Literary Writings. Edited by Margaret A. Simons and Marybeth Timmermann. With a Foreword by Sylvie Le Bon de Beauvoir. The Beauvoir Series. University of Illinois Press, Urbana-Chicago-Springfield 2011.

Beauvoir, Simone de: The Ethics of Ambiguity. Translated from the French by Bernard Frechtman. Citadel Press, New York 2018.

Beer, Gillian: The Common Ground. Essays on Virginia Woolf. Edinburgh University Press, Edinburgh 1996.

Bogic, Anna: 'The Story of the First English Translation of Beauvoir's "Le Deuxième Sexe" And Why It Still Matters', in: SIMONE DE BEAUVOIR STUDIES 2009–2010/26, p. 81–96.

Brooks, Peter: Body Work: Objects of Desire in Modern Narrative. Harvard University Press, Cambridge (MA)-London 1993.

Bugliani, Paolo: '"A Few Loose Sentences": Virginia Woolf e l'eredità meta-saggistica di Montaigne', in: TICONTRE. TEORIA TESTO TRADUZIONE 2018/9, p. 1–26.

Butler, Judith: 'Sex and Gender in Simone de Beauvoir's *Second Sex*', in: YALE FRENCH STUDIES 1986/72, p. 35–49.

Butler, Judith: Gender Trouble. Feminism and the Subversion of Identity. Routledge, New York-London 1999 [1990].

Damásio, António: Descartes' Error: Emotion, Reason, and the Human Brain. Putnam, New York 1994.
Ehrsam, Raphaël: 'Liberté située et sens du monde : Beauvoir et Merleau-Ponty', in: PHILOSOPHIE 2020/1 (N° 144), p. 11–30.
Federici, Silvia: Beyond the Periphery of the Skin: Rethinking, Remaking, and Reclaiming the Body in Contemporary Capitalism. Pm, New York 2020.
Froidevaux-Metterie, Camille: Un Corps à soi. Seuil, Paris 2021.
Fuchs, Thomas: Ecology of the Brain: The Phenomenology and Biology of the Embodied Mind. Oxford University Press, Oxford 2017.
Groenhout, Ruth: 'Beauvoir and The Biological Body', in: Hengehold, Laura / Bauer, Nancy (eds.): *A Companion to Simone de Beauvoir*. Wiley-Blackwell, Chichester-Hoboken 2017, p. 73–86.
Haraway, Donna J.: 'Situated Knowledges: The Science Question in Feminism and the Privilege of Partial Perspective', in: FEMINIST STUDIES 1988/14 (3), p. 575–599.
Haraway, Donna J.: The Companion Species Manifesto: Dogs, People, and Significant Otherness. The Companion Species Manifesto. The University of Chicago Press, Chicago 2003.
Harding, Sandra: 'Rethinking Standpoint Epistemology: What Is "Strong Objectivity?"', in: THE CENTENNIAL REVIEW 1992/36 (3), p. 437–470.
Heinämaa, Sara: Toward a Phenomenology of Sexual Difference: Husserl, Merleau-Ponty, Beauvoir. Rowman & Littlefield, New York 2003.
Jones, Clara: Virginia Woolf. Ambivalent Activist. Edinburgh University Press, Edinburgh 2016.
Karshan, Thomas: 'What is An Essay? Thirteen Answers from Virginia Woolf', in: Karshan, Thomas / Murphy, Kathryn (eds.): *On Essays. Montaigne to the Present*. Oxford University Press, Oxford 2020, p. 31–54.
Kirkpatrick, Kate: Becoming Beauvoir: A Life. Bloomsbury Academic, London 2019.
Mann, Bonnie / FERRARI, Martina (eds.): On ne naît pas femme: on le devient: The Life of a Sentence. Oxford University Press, Oxford 2017.
Merleau-Ponty, Maurice: The Phenomenology of Perception. Translated by Colin Smith, Routledge Classics, Routledge, London-New York 2002.
Moi, Toril: What Is a Woman? and Other Essays. Oxford University Press, Oxford 1999.
Pett, Sarah: 'Rash Reading: Rethinking Virginia Woolf's *On Being Ill*', in: LITERATURE AND MEDICINE 2019/37 (1), p. 26–66.
Snaith, Anna: 'Woolf and Education', in: Fernald, Anne E. (ed.): *The Oxford Handbook of Virginia Woolf*. Oxford University Press, Oxford 2021.
Woolf, Virginia: The Essays of Virginia Woolf. Vol. 4: 1925–1928. Chatto & Windus, London 1994.
Woolf, Virginia: The Essays of Virginia Woolf. Vol. 5: 1929–1932. Chatto & Windus, London 2009.
Woolf, Virginia: The Essays of Virginia Woolf. Vol. 6: 1933–1941. Chatto & Windus, London 2011.
Woolf, Virginia: *A Room of One's Own* and *Three Guineas*, Edited with an Introduction and Notes by Anna Snaith, Oxford World's Classics. Oxford University Press, Oxford 2015.

Silvia Purpuri (University of Trento)

The Welsh/English Tapestry. Bicultural Bilingualism in Dylan Thomas' life and work

> *I like Wales. I am proud to be Welsh.*
> *But I also like being English, and I am proud to be English too*
> (From a BBC radio interview in 1953)

Introduction

Bicultural bilinguals refer to individuals who possess fluency and cultural competence in two distinct languages and corresponding cultures (Grosjean 2015). They have the ability to navigate and effectively communicate in both languages while demonstrating a deep understanding and appreciation of the cultural nuances associated with each. Bicultural bilingualism often stems from personal connections to both cultures, such as through family background, upbringing, or immersion in diverse cultural environments (LaFromboise, Coleman, Gerton 1993). Bicultural bilingual individuals embody the duality of two languages and cultures, seamlessly switching between them and adapting their communication style based on the context (Luna 2008). This bicultural linguistic and cultural competence allows for bridging cultural gaps, fostering cross-cultural understanding, and embracing the richness of multiple linguistic and cultural identities (Grosjean 2015).

Wales, known for its cultural diversity and bilingual heritage, provides a fertile ground to explore the complexities of biculturalism (Williams 2012). This article focuses on the life and work of Dylan Thomas, the renowned Welsh poet, as a case study to examine the interplay between biculturalism and bilingualism. Born in Swansea, Wales, in 1914, Thomas was raised in a Welsh-speaking community, immersed in the vibrant cultural traditions and linguistic diversity of the region (Ferris 2014). This upbringing significantly shaped Thomas' perception of identity, language, and artistic expression. Thomas' language acquisition and cultural identity were deeply influenced by his bilingual environment. Growing up, he encountered both Welsh, the native language of his community, and English, the dominant language of wider communication. This linguistic duality fostered Thomas' bicultural identity, as he embraced elements from both Welsh and English cultures within his work (Davies 2008).

Thomas' poetry serves as a reflection of his bicultural background. Through his works, he artfully intertwines Welsh and English imagery, themes, and linguistic elements, creating a poetic tapestry that blends the influences of both cultures. The fusion of these distinct cultural perspectives allowed Thomas to explore themes of identity, belonging, and nostalgia with a unique depth and complexity (Hallam 2015).

Understanding the impact of bicultural bilingualism on Thomas' artistic expression not only provides insights into his creative process but also offers broader implications for individuals with dual cultural and linguistic backgrounds. Dylan Thomas' life and work offer an intriguing case study to examine the dynamics of bicultural bilingualism. This article aims to shed light on the interconnectedness of language, culture, and creativity, providing a foundation for further research and dialogue in the field of biculturalism. Further research can also explore the experiences of other bicultural individuals within the Welsh context and beyond, enriching our understanding of the influence of biculturalism on language, identity, and artistic expression.

Welsh Historical background

In order to understand Welsh culture in the twentieth century, it is important to grasp the historical forces that shaped it. The Welsh trace their ancestry back to the ancient Celtic peoples who once inhabited much of Western Europe. In the first century BC, Celtic tribes in southern Britain fell under Roman dominion and, like the rest of the Roman Empire, embraced Christianity. As Roman power waned in the late fifth century, waves of Germanic invaders, particularly the Angles and Saxons, arrived in southern Britain and eventually became the English, named after the Angles. By around 800 CE, the remaining Celts were pushed towards the western and northern regions of Britain, where their descendants, including the Cornish in southwest England and the Welsh (alongside the Irish, who also share Celtic heritage), still reside today. Isolated from other Celts, the Welsh developed their unique language and culture, influenced by their English neighbours. The English names for Wales and its people derive from "wealas" meaning "strangers". In the early Middle Ages, the Welsh began calling themselves "Cymry" meaning "compatriots", a term still used today in Welsh (Cymru today means Wales, in Welsh). Despite the progressive anglicization of Wales, strong Celtic elements persisted in the Welsh consciousness. The legendary King Arthur, potentially a Welsh king who resisted the Anglo-Saxon invasion, and the popular Eisteddfod festivals, featuring competitions in poetry, music, and folk dancing, showcase prominent aspects of Welsh culture. Following the Norman conquest, England's rulers pursued the conquest of Wales and achieved it by the late thirteenth century, despite Welsh opposition. In the fifteenth century, Welsh nobleman Henry Tudor became King Henry VII of England, succeeded by his son Henry VIII and granddaughter Elizabeth I. During Henry VIII's reign, the Acts of Union in 1536 and 1543 merged Wales and England into a unified political and administrative system. Since then, England and Wales have remained united. They have shared a common legal system, parliament, and government.

The Senedd, formerly known as the National Assembly for Wales, was established in 1999 following a referendum in Wales. It has the authority to make legislation on specific areas devolved to it, such as health, education, and transportation, while other matters, such as defence and foreign affairs, remain under the control of the UK Parliament in Westminster. The creation of the Senedd represented a decentralisation of power from the UK government to the Welsh government, allowing Wales to have a greater say in its internal affairs while remaining part of the United Kingdom. Therefore, while England and Wales are still politically and administratively united, the establishment of the Senedd marked a significant devolution of powers to Wales.

The completion of the Severn Bridge in 1966 marked a significant milestone in connecting Wales and England with a road link.[1] Prior to the construction of the bridge, the people of Wales and England could only catch glimpses of each other's country from their respective coastlines. This limited interaction and restricted viewpoint often reinforced a sense of separateness and cultural distinction. By providing a direct road link, the bridge became a symbol of unity and cooperation. It enabled people to move freely across the Severn Estuary, bridging the geographical gap and connecting communities on both sides. The bridge created opportunities for cultural exchange, economic growth, and increased social integration. As people travelled back and forth across the bridge, they were exposed to new experiences, traditions, and perspectives, fostering a greater understanding and appreciation of the similarities and shared heritage between the two nations. Additionally, the Severn Bridge served as a catalyst for regional development, attracting investments, and encouraging tourism. The improved accessibility between Wales and England spurred economic activities, such as trade and commuting, benefiting businesses and individuals on both sides of the bridge. The bridge's role as a tourist attraction also helped to promote the regions it connected, as visitors were drawn to the scenic views and unique experience of crossing between two distinct nations.

---

1 https://www.bbc.com/news/uk-wales-37172242.

Bicultural bilingualism in Wales

Wales is a small nation with a long and varied tradition of bilingualism. In the past, a significant portion of the Welsh population exclusively spoke Welsh (Davies 1993), but this monolingual group diminished throughout the 20th century, with only a small percentage remaining by the 1981 census (Williams 1990). In the mid-twentieth century, approximately 30 percent of Welsh individuals were fluent in their native language, while English was progressively dominating their daily existence. While most Welsh speakers in Wales also speak English, feeling more at ease using Welsh, some individuals still prefer Welsh over English for self-expression. Language choice can differ based on the topic and social setting, even within a single conversation.

Globally, bilingualism is a common experience, with one billion people estimated to be learning English at any given time (Pearson 2009, pp, 380–382). Population growth in regions where English is a second language surpasses that of English-speaking areas. Bilinguals outnumber monolinguals worldwide, a trend expected to continue (Hamers, Blanc 2000). However, within the UK, bilingual communities, including those speaking heritage languages like Welsh or immigrant languages from South Asia or Eastern Europe, remain a minority (Higgs, Williams, Dorling 2004). These communities are often concentrated in urban areas, and their language practices have a varied impact on the country as a whole. A 2006 UK school census indicated a rising proportion of students speaking languages other than English at home, with approximately 1 in 7 primary school pupils and 1 in 10 secondary school students having English as a second or additional language.[2]

Welsh biculturalism, with its intertwining of language and culture, holds a special place in the heart of British literature (Jones 2018). The two languages bear the weight of distinct cultural connotations, shaping personal and collective identities in profound ways (Evans 2020). The Welsh language and its vibrant heritage are deeply rooted, carrying a significance that resonates within the hearts of Welsh speakers (Thomas 2019). For bicultural bilinguals, the use of Welsh language often evokes a profound connection to their Welsh identity, while English may evoke a sense of broader societal or global influences (Roberts 2017). The choice of language becomes a heartfelt expression, reflecting not only cultural background and heritage but also the heartfelt emotions of belonging and pride (Griffiths 2021).

"*To be born Welsh is to be born privileged, not with a silver spoon in your mouth, but with music in your blood and poetry in your soul*".[3] Wales, with its rich

---

2 http://news.bbc.co.uk/2/hi/uk_news/education/6597273.stm.
3 Welsh Proverb, also in the poem 'In Passing' (Harris 1967).

heritage and vibrant cultural traditions, offers a unique upbringing that nurtures a profound connection to music and poetry. The Welsh people have inherited a deep appreciation for their ancient language, Cymraeg, as well as the English language, fostering a harmonious coexistence of both linguistic worlds. From the echoing valleys to the resounding coastlines, the Welsh people are ingrained with an innate love for music that intertwines seamlessly with the cadence of their poetic souls. It is through this fusion of language and artistic passion that Welsh-English bicultural bilingualism truly shines.

The Welsh language is very musical[4] and is renowned for its lyrical nature (Davies 1993, p. 34), characterised by harmonious vowel sounds and intricate consonant combinations. This musicality can be attributed to various factors, including the use of vowel length and pitch changes for emphasis, the presence of musical intonation patterns, and the influence of traditional Welsh music on spoken communication.

Within the Welsh-speaking community, there is a concerted effort to revitalise the Welsh language and preserve Welsh cultural traditions (Thomas 2019). Bilingual individuals who actively engage with the Welsh language play a crucial role in this broader cultural revival, and they take pride in their ability to speak and perpetuate the language. Their contribution reflects a commitment to preserving their linguistic heritage and maintaining a strong connection to Welsh culture (Paulston, Chen, Connerty 1993).

Dylan Thomas: Navigating Bilingualism, Cultural Identity, and Literary Expression

Born in Swansea, Wales, in 1914, Thomas was steeped in the rich tapestry of Welsh culture from an early age (Smith 2002). The Welsh language, with its melodic tones and ancient history, resonated deeply within his being (Jones 2010). Although Thomas primarily wrote in English, his exposure to Welsh language and literature undoubtedly influenced his poetic style and wordplay (Williams 2015). His upbringing in a Welsh-speaking community provided a strong foundation for his artistic sensibilities and lyrical craftsmanship (Davies 2008). Dylan Thomas' parents could both speak Welsh but used English in their home. Thomas, therefore, like most of his Welsh contemporaries, grew up speaking and writing only English. Yet Thomas' English is deeply influenced by Welsh rhythms and cadences, which give even his prose writings a distinctive poetic feel.

---

4 https://theconversation.com/how-the-welsh-developed-their-own-form-of-poetry-73299.

According to the biographers David Holbrook (2014) and Andrew Sinclair (1975), Dylan Thomas's sense of personal identity was heavily influenced by the symbolic significance of his name, "Dylan". His father, D.J. Thomas chose the name, which originates from a bardic legend in the Mabinogion (Davies 2007), an ancient Welsh compendium of cultural traditions. In this legend, a magician compelled a virgin to step over a magic wand, resulting in the birth of a male child named Dylan, meaning "sea son". The child then ran into the sea, embracing a fish-like existence in his natural element. Throughout his poetry, Dylan Thomas' work frequently reflects the power and imagery associated with his name. This is exemplified by the well-known concluding lines of his poem "Fern Hill", which are now engraved on a stone plaque in Cwmdonkin Park, his cherished childhood playground: "*Time held me green and dying / Though I sang in my chains like the sea*" (Thomas 1945).

Thomas' upbringing in a bilingual environment significantly influenced his language acquisition and cultural identity. Welsh, the native language of his community, and English, the dominant language of wider communication, both played vital roles in his linguistic development. This linguistic duality fostered Thomas' sense of bicultural identity, wherein he embraced both Welsh and English cultural elements within his work.

Navigating dual linguistic and cultural identities inevitably brought forth challenges and conflicts for Thomas. The tension between Welsh and English influences occasionally surfaced in his work. It was not a matter of choosing one over the other but rather finding a harmonious balance between the two. Thomas grappled with the complexities of preserving his Welsh heritage while engaging with English literary traditions, allowing both to shape his unique poetic vision.

While rooted in Welsh heritage, Thomas recognized the significance of English as a lingua franca. His bilingualism allowed him to bridge the divide between his Welsh identity and the wider literary world. Through his mastery of the English language, he brought the stories and nuances of Wales to a global audience. Thomas' poetic voice transcended linguistic boundaries, captivating readers across cultures and languages.

Thomas' literary work serves as a profound reflection of his bicultural background. In his works, he skilfully juxtaposes Welsh and English imagery, themes, and linguistic elements, creating a poetic tapestry that blends the influences of both cultures (Jones 2018). Through the use of vivid metaphors, evocative language, and a keen sense of place, Thomas brings to life the bicultural experience in Wales, highlighting the beauty and complexity of his linguistic heritage (Williams 2015). His works serve as a vivid portrayal of the linguistic and cultural richness in Wales, offering deep insights into the bicultural experience (Davies 2008).

Dylan Thomas addressed many concerns through his own experiences. He found a "third space of enunciation" (Bhabha 1994, pp. 312–313) where cultural identities could merge and create new meaning. Let's think, for instance, of the first Severn Bridge, which connected Wales and England. Before, people could only see the neighbouring countries from their own coastlines. But with the bridge, a new viewpoint was possible, high above the divisions, allowing for a broader outlook. Thomas was able to observe himself and the world from a place that was neither "self" nor "other", but something different altogether. Thomas had embraced his Welsh literary traditions while also fulfilling the expectations of English society as a romantic poet. Despite the challenges he faced due to linguistic dominance, he found harmony within himself and expressed it in his work, such as the play *Under Milk Wood*. Through literature, Dylan Thomas became the one defining his identity, rather than being defined by others (Powell 2011).

Under Milk Wood

Under Milk Wood combines voices, sights, and sounds to portray a day in the life of a fictional Welsh seaside village. The play, also known as "A Play for Voices", showcases Thomas' talent as both a radio writer and a poet. It presents a polyphonic narrative that visits the inhabitants of Llareggub as they sleep, wake up, and go about their daily activities until nightfall.

Thomas skilfully balances rhythmic and poetic language with an ear for the musicality of speech, for which the Welsh language and the Welsh accents are famous for, creating a charming and humorous play that depicts a community responding to the arrival of spring in a mythical and deeply textured way. While the play exudes warmth and affection, it also carries a more serious undertone influenced by the aftermath of World War II. Its affirming and redemptive nature reflects Thomas' belief in the regenerative innocence and grace of ordinary people.

One of the notable aspects of Under Milk Wood is the blending of different cultures, where Dylan Thomas combines his Welsh and English influences to create something unique. It is a play about hybridity as it blends different cultures, languages, and perspectives, showcasing the rich diversity found in Llareggub. Dylan Thomas combines his Welsh and English influences to create a unique linguistic fusion that reflects the multicultural nature of the play's setting. The characters speak a blend of Welsh and English, incorporating local dialects and idioms. The play challenges the idea of cultural centrality by reversing perspectives and giving voice to marginalised characters, representing various social classes and backgrounds. The narrative structure of the play, resembling a poetic radio drama, allows for a multiplicity of voices and emphasises diversity within the community.

The play is meant to be heard rather than seen, similar to the radio broadcasts Thomas wrote for the BBC. It reflects the idea of multiple voices and narratives, with characters engaging in dialogue and exchanges with each other and the audience. Thomas uses parody, humour, and a fictional village setting to portray life in Wales. The play also challenges the idea of being either at the centre or marginalised by reversing perspectives through its characters in a diverse universe (Powell 2011).

Llareggub becomes a space where eccentricities are accepted, sins are forgiven, and love is nurtured, or at least imagined and desired. Thomas demonstrates compassion for the everyday dramas of life and believes that shared experiences bring people together. Each character is vividly brought to life through Thomas' generous and affectionate portrayal. Notable characters include Captain Cat, Myfanwy Price, Organ Morgan, Willy Nilly Postman, Polly Garter, Dai Bread, and others.

The town of Llareggub itself possesses a collective personality divided between a conscious world of daily activities narrated by the First Voice and a subconscious world of intimate thoughts and emotions revealed by the Second Voice. Beneath the town's calm exterior, powerful and often sexual forces are at play. The Second Voice exposes secret fantasies, such as Gossamer Beynon feeling Sinbad Sailor's *"goatbeard tickle her in the middle of the world"* (Thomas 1954, p. 47) or Mr. Pugh imagining poisoning his wife with deadly nightshade. Each character's relationship follows peculiar rules, but they all remain deeply entangled in their own perceptions of love.

In Thomas' world, these sensuous relationships cannot be detached from the shadow of death. Polly Garter, who engages in promiscuity, sings all day about her lost love, Little Willy Wee. Mrs. Ogmore-Pritchard can only tolerate a deceased husband, and blind Captain Cat is haunted by the memory of Rosie Probert, *"the one love of his sea-life"* (Thomas 1954, p. 51). Many characters struggle with their unfulfilled and sometimes explicit desires.

Under Milk Wood is a sensitive and often comedic exploration of Welsh life, portraying its people as uniquely blessed. They are the *"chosen people of His kind fire in Llareggub's land"* (Thomas 1954, p. 62) and despite their flaws, the town retains its magic and sacred significance. The characters in the play embrace the Welsh language as an essential part of their identity, reinforcing a sense of community and cultural resilience (Williams 2015). Thomas' depiction of small seaside places in his work is rooted in his personal experiences and takes us to locations that he had personal access to. While the existence of Llareggub (which interestingly translates to 'bugger all' when read backwards) as a specific real place is uncertain, it is more likely that Thomas drew inspiration from his own encounters in rural Welsh coastal towns, particularly those along the Gower coastline where he spent his formative years. Examples of such places include Mumbles, a town inhabited by retired seamen and other colourful characters during Thomas' time, as well as New Quay, where he resided with his family in the mid-1940s. Furthermore, Laugharne, his final home until his death, also likely influenced his portrayal of these coastal towns (Thomas 2014). These locations, where Thomas spent significant periods of time, likely influenced his portrayal of the coastal towns in the play. The fictitious town of Llareggub, which may be based on Welsh coastal towns like Mumbles, New Quay, and Laugharne, represents the Welsh cultural experience. The First Voice, speaking from the author's omniscient perspective, offers insights into the bilingual and bicultural nature of the town.

In terms of bicultural bilingualism, the play portrays a dichotomy between characters who are insular, centred solely around Llareggub, and those who have a broader worldview. The characters like Mrs Ogmore-Pritchard, Polly Garter, and Nogood Boyo demonstrate a parochial existence, while characters like Captain Cat and Reverend Eli Jenkins show an awareness of the wider world. While the town's inhabitants focus on their everyday concerns, these characters exist on the margins and possess a broader perspective. Captain Cat, a retired blind sea-captain, represents a character with a broader perspective and is able to see beyond the illusions of the town. Although physically blind, he can still sense the town's activities and has travelled the world. His experience parallels Plato's allegory of The Cave, where he has glimpsed a greater reality but is considered blind by those who haven't shared his insights (Law 2007, p. 78). Reverend Eli Jenkins represents the Welsh cultural heritage. He recites Welsh poetry and is knowledgeable about Welsh history. He embodies a sense of double-consciousness, living both within the town of Llareggub and in touch with a wider cultural identity. He represents the Welsh heritage and language through his use of Welsh words and references to Welsh history.

The play captures the linguistic tapestry of Welsh biculturalism, showcasing the rich cultural heritage and intermingling of languages within Welsh society. Dylan Thomas presents characters who effortlessly switch between Welsh and English, showcasing the linguistic and cultural duality of Welsh biculturalism. For instance, the above-mentioned Captain Cat seamlessly integrates Welsh phrases into his English dialogue, emphasising the fusion of Welsh and English within his bicultural identity. Another example of Thomas' bicultural reflection can be found in the opening lines of this poem. Through rich and descriptive language, he captures the essence of the Welsh landscape and its people. He writes:

> It is spring, moonless night in the small town, starless and bible-black, the cobblestreets silent and the hunched, courters'-and-rabbits' wood limping invisible down to the sloeblack, slow, black, crowblack, fishing boat-bobbing sea (Thomas 1954, p. 1).

This quote demonstrates Thomas' skilful use of imagery and linguistic elements. The phrase "*starless and bible-black*" conveys a sense of mystery and darkness, while poetically evoking nighttime in the tiny, darkened village, and the repetition of words such as "*black*" and "*slow*" adds a musicality to the language, reminiscent of the lyrical qualities often found in Welsh poetry. (The phrase "*courters'-and-rabbits' wood*" refers to Milk Wood, which stands near the town and attracts courting couples; sloe berries are deep black in colour).

Under Milk Wood serves as a compelling testament to the profound bicultural bilingualism that shapes the Welsh cultural experience. Through a polyphonic narrative and the seamless integration of languages, the play captures the duality and interconnectedness of Welsh society. Characters effortlessly switch between Welsh and English, exemplifying the fluidity of their bicultural identities. Thomas's portrayal of Llareggub, drawing inspiration from Welsh coastal towns, becomes a vibrant canvas where the fusion of languages reinforces a sense of community and cultural resilience. Dylan Thomas skilfully weaves together various contrasts and dualities, including the good and the bad, the conscious and the subconscious, the insular and the worldly, and the humorous and the serious. Through his polyphonic narrative, Thomas creates a vibrant tapestry of voices, sights, and sounds that reflect the complex nature of human experience. The play celebrates the blending of cultures and languages, capturing the essence of Welsh biculturalism and highlighting the interconnectedness of communities. Under Milk Wood is a testament to Thomas' belief in the resilience and grace of ordinary people, affirming the regenerative power of shared experiences and the inherent beauty found within the multifaceted dimensions of life.

Legacy and Influence. Implications and future directions

Dylan Thomas's contribution to literature extends far beyond his own lifetime. His Welsh-English identity and poetic genius continue to resonate with readers around the world. The interplay between his linguistic and cultural heritage laid the foundation for a unique artistic voice that defies borders. Thomas's ability to reconcile and celebrate both aspects of his identity inspires individuals grappling with their own bilingual and bicultural experiences.

The study of bicultural bilingualism in the context of Dylan Thomas' life and work provides valuable insights into the broader implications for individuals with dual cultural and linguistic backgrounds. Understanding the complexities, challenges, and creative possibilities that arise from biculturalism can contribute to fostering a more inclusive and appreciative society. Further research should explore the experiences of other bicultural individuals within the Welsh context and beyond, broadening our understanding of the impact of biculturalism on language, identity, and artistic expression.

Conclusion

It was T.S. Eliot who once described a great poet as someone who, in writing their own experience, was able to write the experience of their time (Wisker 2007, p. 3). In his play 'Under Milk Wood', Dylan Thomas not only captured his own position of being caught between the cultures of Wales and England in his drama but also managed to recreate the state of confusion many of his generation felt in searching for their own cultural identity. These individuals, also known as "Anglo-Welsh", were neither truly Welsh nor truly English, living in the language of England while being people of Wales. However, Welsh language writers such as Saunders Lewis considered them inauthentic, labelling them as the "un-Welsh product of English linguistic colonisation" (Goodby, Wigginton 2019, p. 8) and accusing them of turning their backs on the Welsh language, which they believed was essential to Welsh identity. Lewis's puritanical attitude toward national identity denied the hyphenated identities claimed by individuals like Thomas, asserting that they belonged to the English. In the midst of this dispute over splitting hairs, it is unsurprising that Thomas found solace in writing.

Dylan Thomas' life and work exemplify the intricate dance between linguistic and cultural identities. His Welsh heritage, combined with his fluency in English, provided a multifaceted lens through which he viewed the world. Thomas' ability to weave together the threads of Welsh and English influences produced a poetic tapestry that continues to captivate and inspire. His legacy serves as a testament to the richness and depth of embracing diverse linguistic and cultural identities, forging a path towards a more inclusive and harmonious world.

Dylan Thomas' life and work serve as a compelling case study for exploring the dynamics of bicultural bilingualism in Wales. By delving into his background, language acquisition, and artistic expression, this article sheds light on the interconnectedness of language, culture, and creativity. The study of bicultural bilingualism has broader implications for understanding the complexities of identity and the potential for artistic expression in multilingual societies, paving the way for further research and dialogue in this field.

Works Cited

Ackerman, J.: Dylan Thomas: his life and work. Springer, New York 2016.
Bhanha, H.K.: The Location of Culture, Routledge, London 1994.
Davies, J.: The Welsh Language. University of Wales Press, Bath 1993.
Davies, J.: Language Planning in Wales: Fifty Years of Social Change. University of Wales Press, Bath 2008.
Davies, R.: Dylan Thomas and the Welsh Literary Tradition. University of Wales Press, Bath, 2008.
Davies, S. (ed.).: The Mabinogion. Oxford University Press, Oxford 2007.
Evans, D.: 'Language and Culture in Welsh Biculturalism: A Sociolinguistic Perspective', in: JOURNAL OF MULTILINGUALISM AND MULTICULTURALISM 2020/32(4), pp. 205–221.
Ferris, P.: Dylan Thomas: A Biography. Overlook Press, Woodstock, NY 2014.
Goodby, J. / Wigginton, C. (eds.): Dylan Thomas. Bloomsbury, London 2019.
Griffiths, L.: 'Language Choice as a Reflection of Cultural Identity and Pride among Bicultural Bilinguals', in: JOURNAL OF SOCIOLINGUISTICS 2021/28(2), pp. 87–103.
Grosjean, F.: 'Bicultural Bilinguals', in: INTERNATIONAL JOURNAL OF BILINGUALISM 2015/19(5), pp. 572–586.
Hallam, T. '"Curse, bless, me now": Dylan Thomas and Saunders Lewis', in: JOURNAL OF THE BRITISH ACADEMY 2015/3, pp. 211–253.
Hamers, J.F. / Blanc, M. / Blanc, M.H. / Hamers, J.F.: Biliguality and Bilingualism. Cambridge University Press, Cambridge 2000.
Harris, B.: In Passing (poem), 1967.
Higgs, G. / Williams, C. / Dorling, D.: 'Use of the Census of Population to Discern Trends in the Welsh Language: An Aggregate Analysis', in: AREA 2004/36(2), pp. 187–201.
Holbrook, D.: Dylan Thomas: The Code of Night. Bloomsbury, London 2014.
Jones, M.: 'The Influence of Welsh Language and Culture on Dylan Thomas', in: WELSH JOURNAL OF LITERARY STUDIES 2010/17(2), pp. 45–63.
Jones, A.: 'Welsh Biculturalism and its Significance in British Literature', in: JOURNAL OF BRITISH LITERARY STUDIES 2018/45(2), pp. 78–93.
LaFromboise, T. / Coleman, H.L.K / Gerton, J.: 'Psychological Impact of Biculturalism: Evidence and Theory, in: PSYCHOL. BULL. 1993/114, pp. 395–412.
Law, S.: Philosophy, DK Publishing, London 2007.
Luna, D. et Al.: 'One Individual, Two Identities: Frame Switching among Biculturals', in: JOURNAL OF CONSUMER RESEARCH 2008/0(0), pp. 33–52.
Paulston, C.B. / Chen, P.C. / Connerty, M.C.: 'Language Regenesis: A Conceptual Overview of Language Revival, Revitalisation and Reversal', in: JOURNAL OF MULTILINGUAL & MULTICULTURAL DEVELOPMENT 1993/14(4), pp. 275–286.
Pearson, B.Z.: Children with Two Languages. The Cambridge Handbook of Child Language. Cambridge University Press, Cambridge 2009.
Phinney, J.S. / Devich-Navarro, M.: 'Variations in Bicultural Identification among African American and Mexican American Adolescents', in: JOURNAL OF RESEARCH ON ADOLESCENCE 1997/7(1), pp. 3–32.
Powell, K.: 'One Foot in Wales and My Vowels in England': Double-Consciousness in the Work of Dylan Thomas. Thesis, University of Notre Dame Australia 2011.

Roberts, G. 'Bilingualism and Identity: Exploring the Welsh Experience', in: INTERNATIONAL JOURNAL OF BILINGUAL EDUCATION AND BILINGUALISM 2017/20(1), pp. 45–62.
Sinclair, A. / Thomas D.: No Man More Magical. Holt, Rinehart & Winston, New York 1975.
Smith, R.: Dylan Thomas: A Biography. Oxford University Press, Oxford 2002.
Thomas, D.: Fern Hill (poem), 1945.
Thomas, D.: Under Milk Wood (poem), 1954.
Thomas, D.: The Collected Poems of Dylan Thomas: The Centenary Edition. Hachette UK, London 2014.
Thomas, E.: 'The Significance of the Welsh Language in Welsh Cultural Identity', in: JOURNAL OF LANGUAGE AND CULTURE 2019/17(3), pp. 112–127.
Williams, D.: 'Language and Style in the Poetry of Dylan Thomas: A Linguistic Analysis', in: JOURNAL OF WELSH LITERATURE 2015/22(1), pp. 78–94.
Williams, R.: Border Country. Parthian Books, Cardigan 2012.
Williams, C.H.: 'The Anglicisation of Wales', in: Coupland, N. (ed.): *English in Wales: Diversity, Conflict, and Change*. Multilingual Matters, Clevedon 1990, pp. 38–41.
Whisker, A.: T.S. Eliot: A Beginner's Guide. Hodder & Stroughton, Oxon 2007.

Web Sources

BBC. https://www.bbc.com/news/uk-wales-37172242.
BBC. http://news.bbc.co.uk/2/hi/uk_news/education/6597273.stm.
The Conversation: https://theconversation.com/how-the-welsh-developed-their-own-form-of-poetry-73299.

Paola Della Valle (University of Torino)

From Page to Screen: Undermining Nazi Propaganda in *Caging Skies* and *Jojo Rabbit*

Drawing inspiration from pre-existing stories has always been a common practice for writers and artists, in past and present times. Filmmakers, too, were inspired by literary texts, which could not only provide well-devised plots but also offer a way to prove the potentials of the new medium. The adaptation of literary works and famous classics was in fact a means to claim the right for the cinema to be considered a real art form, instead of merely the result of technological progress or part of the entertainment industry (Cartmell, and Whelehan 2010, p. 28). However, it also opened these films to significant criticism from both the literary and cinematic world.

The interaction between literature and cinematography has been the object of much research since the birth of the seventh art.[1] In the first half of 20th century monographs on this topic were written by directors and film theorists such as Sergei Eisenstein, Bela Balázs, Louis Delluc and many others. A remarkable contribution to the study of screen adaptation was certainly André Bazin's essay 'Adaptation, of the Cinema as Digest', published in 1948. He criticised the preoccupation with "fidelity" that animated the critical debate of his time and eliminated the hierarchy between the source text and its adaptation. In his view, adaptations and their source texts were destined to be seen as separate manifestations of a single work:

> The (literary?) critic of the year 2050 would find not a novel out of which a play and film had been "made," but rather a single work reflected through three art forms, an artistic pyramid with three sides, all equal in the eyes of the critic. The "work" would then be only an ideal point at the top of this figure, which itself is an ideal construct. (Bazin 2014, p. 26).

---

1 Cinema is called the seventh art together with drama, as both involve acting. The other arts are: architecture, music, painting, sculpture, poetry, and dance.

Bazin questions the traditional concepts of work and author: the former is almost transformed into an immaterial entity and the latter can no longer be defined as a single unity. Moreover, as James Naremore pinpoints:

> Bazin asks us to think of film adaptation in relation to commercialism, industrial modernity, and democracy, and to compare it with an engraving or digest that makes the so-called original "readily accessible to all." […] He also observes that adaptation has a number of important social functions, one of which is directly pedagogical, taking the form of everything from 19th-century "abridged" classics to more recent things Bazin does not mention, such as *Classics Illustrated* comics, *Reader's Digest* condensed books, and plot summarys [sic] in *Cliff Notes*. (Naremore 1999, p. 10).

Bazin attacks an elitist view of culture, the cliché according to which culture is inseparable from intellectual effort, and the distinction between highbrow and lowbrow. He is in fact able to predict the future of adaptation in the world of mass cultural production, as Naremore recognizes:

> Whatever the case may be, it is high time that writers on adaptation recognize what Bazin saw in 1948. The study of adaptation needs to be joined with the study of recycling, remaking, and every other form of retelling in the age of mechanical reproduction and electronic communication. By this means, adaptation will become part of a general theory of repetition and will move from the margins to the center of contemporary media studies. (Naremore 1999, p. 11).

Another step away from fidelity occurs in George Bluestone's 1957 book, *Novels into Film*, considered the first academic monograph on film adaptation. Bluestone argues that fidelity is impossible to achieve, because change is inevitable the moment one abandons the linguistic for the visual medium (Bluestone 1957, p. 5). So novels "metamorphose" into another medium, which has its own formal or narratological possibilities.

A similar point is later made by Robert Stam. He underlines that the language of criticism dealing with the film adaptation of novels has often used highly moralistic terms such as *"infidelity, betrayal, deformation, violation, vulgarization,* and *desecration,* each accusation carrying its specific charge of outraged negativity" (Stam 2000, p. 54). Fidelity is however not only impossible but even undesirable. This is due to the inevitable passage from a "single-track, uniquely verbal medium such as the novel" to a "multi-track medium such as film" (p. 56), based on the interplay of moving photographic images, music, sound effects, and theatrical performance. Looking for the ontological essence of the original source in the adaptation is useless. The focus, Stam says, should be on the "diacritical specificity" (p. 59) of the medium, deriving from its materials of expression Moreover, he underlines the nature of the literary text as an open (not closed) structure (or better "structuration", as the latter Roland Barthes would have it) (p. 57), that is, able to generate a plethora of possible readings. The question that consequently arises is: "fidelity to what?" (p. 57). While denying any form of superiority of the literary text over its film adaptation, Stam reflects on other possible "tropes" rather than fidelity to signify adaptation, such as: "translation, reading, dialogization, cannibalization, transmutation, transfiguration and signifying" (p. 62). The best formula, in the end, seems to be that of adaptation as an ongoing "intertextual dialogical process": "The concept of intertextual dialogism suggests that every text forms an intersection of textual surfaces. [...] Intertextuality, then, helps us transcend the aporias of "fidelity"" (64).

The pervasive force of the concept of fidelity has led many critics throughout the second half of the 20th to explore the topic of "literature and cinema" by comparing a text with its film adaptation or by comparing various screen adaptations of the same text in search of possible objective laws or rules underlying the passage from one medium to another (Kuryaev / Osmukhina 2018, p. 377). However, this is not a homogeneous process and includes various types of transformations of the original texts. In their recent overview of the literature concerning film adaptations of literary texts, Kuryaev and Osmukhina come to the conclusion that:

> To date, neither the theory of cinema, nor literary studies have developed scientific instruments of analysis, which would objectively compare the literary work and its cinematic version. At the same time there is a need in the development of scientific criteria for assessing the screen adaptation of literary works. (Kuryaev / Osmukhina 2018, p. 378).

Interestingly, they underline that the need to develop methodological considerations for comparing screen adaptations and their literary sources should concern literary criticism as well as film studies. In fact, literary critics should not only aim to evaluate the "adequacy" of the film adaptation, since the cinematic interpretation contributes to the history of the reception of the literary text and is therefore involved in the formation of literary history. In their view, any film adaptation can be considered a further variant in the reading of the literary text, but, being an independent aesthetic product, it also becomes a continuation of the literary text's history (p. 380). Moreover, through screenings the cinema not only acquaints the wider public with a certain literary text but also contributes to preventing its "necrosis" (p. 376). In their conclusions, the spirit of Bazin's landmark article seems to resonate.

Most importantly, Kuryaev and Osmukhina's perspective also reflects the notion of intermediality, that is, the belief that today any artistic expression cannot emerge in isolation but only in dialogue with other forms of art. The word "intermedia" was coined by Dick Higgins at the end of 1965 to describe art forms that draw on several media, growing into new hybrids. As explained by Friedman and Diaz, this concept underlines the impossibility, today, of tracing borders between art and life or between different types of art:

> Intermedia works cross the boundaries of recognized media, often fusing the boundaries of art with media that have not previously been considered art forms. Higgins (1966a, 1969a, p. 11–29, 2001) published a now-legendary essay describing an art form appropriate to artists who feel that there are no boundaries between art and life. Along with many artists and composers, Higgins felt the time had come to erase the boundaries between art and life. From this, it followed that there could be few boundaries between art forms, perhaps none, and that new forms of art could enter the previously distinct media from the larger life-world. (Friedman / Diaz 2018, p. 27–28).

An original contribution to the discourse of cinematic adaptations of literary texts, going again in the direction of a "scientific" systematization, was provided by Zinnatullina et al in 2019. They trace a sort of loose taxonomy of film adaptations according to an "algorithm", namely, the different formula or format that is used. However, their theory also accounts for the interdependence and mutual influence of the two media, thus affirming the idea of intermediality in the arts. According to them there are three types of algorithms.

The first and most used one can be expressed as "literary work-scenario-screen version". This kind has been used since the very beginning of cinematic adaptations. An example is the 20-minute short film *Robinson Crusoe* directed in 1902 by French director George Melies. The screen version does not strictly correspond to the primary source because its main goal is to transfer the sense of the literary text using film language and sometimes adding something new. The viewer will estimate any screen work from the perspective of how it corresponds to the level of the primary source. A good screen version gives viewers a chance to experience what they admired and what touched them in the book. It visualizes what they could imagine when reading.

The second algorithm is expressed as "literary work-scenario-screen version-literary work" and occurs in cyclic works. Some elements of the movie can be incorporated in the literary work when the screen version of one part of the book is being produced simultaneously with the process of writing another part. This happened, for example, in the cycle about Harry Potter. The moment of the release of the first movie *Harry Potter and the Sorcerer's Stone* (2001) coincided with the time of writing of the fifth volume *Harry Potter and the Order of the Phoenix*, which was influenced by the film. For example, the characters of Lee Jordan and Angelina Johnson acquire new details in the book that reflect the features of the actors in the film.

The third algorithm can be defined as "scenario-movie-literary work" or novelization. This formula implies that a certain idea is translated into a film and only later into a book. Novelisation basically arises from three different situations. First it may happen when films were planned or shot but not shown on screens, as for example Francis Ford Coppola's *Megalopolis* or Stanley Kubrick's *Napoleon: The Greatest Movie Never Made*. Both projects were never released on the big screen and ended up being published in book form. The second situation occurs when a book is published as an expanded version of a successful movie with new episodes and additional information, and may become a sort of promotion of the movie itself. An example is Jane Campion's book *The Piano* (1993), that came out after the film. The third situation reflects books that were inspired by films, like Anthony Burgess's novel *Man of Nazareth* inspired by Zeffirelli's movie, or books originating from the director's dissatisfaction with the film and the need to rewrite it in book form, as for the re-writing of the 1996 series *Neverwhere* by Neil Gaiman (published in 2009).

Jojo Rabbit (2019) – Jewish-Māori Taika Waititi's film adaptation of the bestselling novel *Caging Skies* (2019) by the New Zealand-Italian-Belgian author Christine Leunens – follows the first algorithm, the most traditional one ("literary work-scenario-screen version") and succeeds in catching the primary meaning of the book, despite the relevant alterations in its plot. The film can also be viewed as a new artwork, an independent manifestation of the original text, a "side of the pyramid" in Bazin's terms, which emphasizes one major aspect of the novel: the mix of ridiculous and tragic in Nazi rhetorical propaganda and the incapacity of people to see it.

The story is set in Vienna, after Austria's annexation as a province of the Third Reich, and is narrated through the eyes of Johannes Betzler, an enthusiastic boy and member first of the *Jungvolk* and then of the *Hitlerjugend* (the junior and senior sections of the Hitler Youth). The military training and Nazi indoctrination imposed on Austrian youth are treated ironically in both the book and the film, as a result of the unreliable narrator's naïve perspective. The two texts also insist on the gap between the detached and critical attitude of the protagonist's family towards the Nazi discourse and the tragicomic fanaticism of the indoctrinated boy. The situation however changes when Johannes (called Jojo in the movie) discovers that his family is hiding a Jewish girl, Elsa Kor, and ends up falling in love with her. The development of this "forbidden" love, according to the Nazi anti-Semitic view, however, takes different paths in the novel and the screen adaptation.

The main difference between book and film is that the former covers a longer period of Johannes' life, from infancy to adulthood. Johannes' attachment to Elsa turns into a morbid love and an almost implausible situation. Fearing that Elsa may leave him once the war is over, he lies to her that the Germans have won the war and that she must continue to live in hiding. Maintaining the lie in post-war Austria takes ingenuity, a kind of desperate creativity that absorbs all his energy and prevents him from developing fruitful social and job relations, causing the protagonist's total isolation and destitution. The second part of the novel, therefore, focuses on how the couple become trapped for a long time in a toxic bond that continuously risks strangling them, making them alternatively the victim and the persecutor. As Anil Menon underlines in his review, "*Caging Skies* is the story of an ordinary man who commits an unforgiveable act in the name of love" (Menon 2020). Menon also justly underlines the particular quality of the writer's restrained prose in the first person, suitable to convey the protagonist's deviant psyche, and describes the Kafkaesque atmosphere that pervades the story:

> Leunens' style is tailored to suit the stolid and not particularly self-aware mind of Johannes. [...] The one attempt at poetic writing is in the prologue where Johannes compares his lie to the planting of a great tree. It's not an apt metaphor. A tree is the very emblem of nature's nobility. What Johannes has constructed isn't a tree of lies, but rather a Kafkaesque burrow, in which he doesn't recognise that the enemy he strains to hear and barricade and protect Elsa against is himself. (Menon 2020).

On the other hand, the film mainly concentrates on dismantling the power of Nazi propaganda by exploiting the comic potentialities of its rhetoric and indoctrination methods, and by showing their inconsistencies once the boy's perspective changes. In particular, a new important character is added: Jojo's imaginary friend, Adolf Hitler, played by the film director himself, Taika Waititi. The colonisation of the boy's mind by this invasive presence is made visible on the screen: an effective overwhelming influence demonstrating the successful work of Nazi education in manipulating young generations. Being a projection of fluctuating moods in an infantile personality, the imaginary friend can be bossy or paternalistic, reproachful or consolatory, but also joyful and exhilarating. Waititi expands and develops, in fact, a minor reference in the novel to Johannes' internalisation of Hitler as an imaginary friend, when his alliance with the *Führer* is menaced by the rise of his interest in the Jewish girl:

> If it's true I'd tried to get the young woman off my mind, by that time I was also trying to get Adolf Hitler off it. His constant reproach about my shortcomings irked me: my incapability, indecorum, infidelity, all starting with *in* and ejecting me *out* of his good opinion. Whenever I came across a picture of him in a magazine, father figure that he was, my insides contracted and I quickly turned the page. (Leunens 2019, p. 72).

Going back to Leunens' work, Menon writes that "the novel is framed as a confession, a sort of aborted Bildungsroman" (2020) and defines it "darkly comic". In point of fact, *Caging Skies* is a counter-Bildungsroman illustrating not the evolution but the regression of the protagonist, unable to escape from the parallel world in which he has taken refuge after the crash of his previous beliefs. As Menon underlines: "In post-WW II Vienna, Johannes is leaderless, jobless, war-mutilated, and without anything to look forward to" (Menon 2020). Elsa thus becomes the totalizing object of his attention: without a family (they die throughout the novel) or a social network to contain his paranoid mind, he cultivates the myth of himself as a hero, who is hiding and protecting the girl from a Nazi anti-Semitic society. The fake life he has constructed for himself and Elsa will cause his economic ruin, self-isolation and psychological collapse.

In the filmic text, on the contrary, there is a positive evolution of the protagonist, although he physically remains the same boy (the actor Roman Griffin Davis) throughout the whole story. The closer Jojo gets to the Jewish girl, the more his blind fanaticism is brought into question until it turns into a sense of solidarity and complicity. The audience witness the decolonisation of his imagery, once occupied by Nazi rhetoric, and the gradual replacement of it with a new narrative: the imagery of romantic love. If Jojo does not really grow up physically, he evolves as a human being. Waititi is able to transform the story into an effective critique of Germany's Nazi regime without falling into dark tragedy, even in the most serious scenes of the film, like the death of Jojo's mother (performed by Scarlett Johansson), hanged in the square with other anti-Nazi partisans, or the final battle between the Allied liberation forces and the German troops. By using a boy's point of view and his childish imagination, the film produces that detachment that allows social commentary, satire, and real comedy, recalling Roberto Benigni's *La vita è bella* (*Life is Beautiful*), a Chaplinesque fable about the power of imagination, set first against the stark reality of Italy during the fascist period and then in a German concentration camp during the Second World War.

Many dark realistic details and episodes included in the novel are cut in the film or transformed into grotesque scenes that convey the message but diminish the charge of violence. Johannes' nickname "Rabbit" is not mentioned in the book but refers to a precise episode during one of the compulsory special camps with the *Hitlerjugend*. In the novel Johannes is ordered to kill a duck with his bare hands by twisting its neck, in the film the duck is replaced by a rabbit. The episode, in both book and film, represents the boy's first impact with death by killing – that is, the actual killing of a living being – and the first act of blind obedience to demonstrate his cold Aryan virility. Johannes is however, shocked and starts having some thoughtful re-considerations on the extent to which people should be faithful to Hitler, as appears in this extract from the book reporting a conversation with his friend Kippi:

> Kippi asked me afterward, if I had to kill him for the Führer, could I? I looked at him and his face was so familiar. I knew I wouldn't have been able to; and neither would he have been able to kill me. But we both agreed this wasn't good–we were weak, and would have to work on it. Ideally, a leader told us, we should be able to hit a baby's head against the wall and not feel anything. Feelings were mankind's most dangerous enemy. They above

all were what must be killed if we were to make ourselves a better people. (Leunens 2019, p. 43).

In the film Jojo, too, is reluctant to kill the trembling and soft animal in his hands and finally runs away, thus gaining the derogatory nickname of Jojo Rabbit.

In the book. Johannes' blind faith in Hitler is also shaken when his best friend Kippi dies during a military camp, an episode that does not happen in the film:

> One second Kippi was standing there, the next he was replaced by a mound of dirt that looked like an absurd improvised tomb.
> If only he could have come back to life, we could have split our sides laughing about it; but without Kippi I didn't laugh or talk much to anybody anymore. It was the beginning of an irrepressible loneliness, of walking around with a big old hole in my gut. (Leunens 2019, p. 47).

Actually, in the film Kippi is replaced by the chubby figure of Yorki (Archie Yates), Jojo's buddy, who provides most of the comic lines in the film and constitutes another example of unreliable commentator of the historical scene. Both Jojo and Yorki will survive.

Another major difference is when Johannes is severely injured in a raid during military service and he loses part of his left cheekbone and forearm, which he cannot move any longer. In the film, he has just some scars and is neither disfigured nor mutilated. Moreover, while the book deals with a whole family (father, mother, grandmother, a dead sister) and a network of external relationships, offering an accurate picture of the 1940s Viennese bourgeoisie against its economic and historical background, in the film Jojo lives with his mother only. He believes his father is a soldier fighting on the front, but he later discovers he is actually a partisan of the resistance groups sprung up against the Nazi regime. His mother, too, is working secretly against the German occupation and will pay a high price for it, as mentioned before.

If the details about the family and its entourage are reduced on the screen, there are some characters that conversely don't appear in the book but only in the film, since they are functional to symbolize the Nazi discourse. Fraulein Rahm (Rebel Wilson), for example, is the epitome of the Teutonic, corpulent, blonde Aryan woman, totally identified with the gender discourse of the Nazi regime: a mother of eighteen children, willing to sacrifice them to the *Führer*; a teacher at the *Hitlerjugend* camp, encouraging all sorts of obnoxious fantasies about the Jews and the other "enemies" of the regime; and an unscrupled fighter, pushing minors into the battle-camp to die. The exaggerated behaviour of the woman turns her into a grotesque and comical character. She represents the most acritical and stupid fanaticism of an adult who has ingested the Nazi propaganda in its most tragi-comical aspects. Another new character and example of faithful executioner is Captain Deertz, the Gestapo officer that comes to search Jojo's house. Interestingly, this part is played by two-metre-tall actor Stephan Merchant, whose top-down gaze is continuously emphasised by the camera, perfectly conveying the strict and omnipresent control of the Nazi political police. Finally, the surreal figure of Captain Klezendorf represents a counter-image of the regime. He is presented first as a cow-boy, then as visibly gay and insubordinate soldier, eventually as an aesthete rather than a military, who designs his own extravagant uniform to participate in the last battle as though he wanted to make himself an artwork and be remembered this way. The scene of the battle itself alternates realistic and violent images to grotesque and hilarious ones. Klezendorf will be fully rehabilitated at the very end, when he puts his life at stake to save Jojo.

An interesting example of how the film maintains and translates a central concept of the book into images, that is, a passage from one medium to another, is provided by Johannes's induced view of the Jews. In the book we read that the Jews were represented by Nazi propaganda as living monsters, who loved ugliness and perversity, as demonstrated by the paintings of (probably) avant-garde Jewish artists that the boys were shown at school:

> We learned, too, how Jews were unable to love beauty and instead preferred ugliness. Again and again we were shown paintings they had created and admired–ugly works where a person's eye was not in the right place but in front of his face, paintings where hands looked like the bloated udder of a cow, where hips joined directly with breasts, where subjects had no neck, no waist. (Leunens 2019, p. 45).

In *Jojo Rabbit*, Waititi translates this idea on the screen by first showing how Fraulein Rahm encourages her young disciples to think of the Jews as the devil's children, with horns, snake tongues and fish scales, then by depicting the first appearance of Elsa (actress Thomasin McKenzie) as an animal creeping out of its den, her body dismembered by the camera that first zooms in on her fingers, clinging to the doorjamb as claws. Slowly the camera zooms out to show a terrified Jojo getting the entire image of the girl. Another example of translation of words or concepts into images is the comical use of the greeting "Heil Hitler" in the film, becoming a mechanical and senseless repetition similar to a refrain or a silly game.

Novel and film dismantle, step by step, the protagonist's ideals fabricated by Nazi propaganda, and gradually show the gap between ideology and reality. In the film, however, this process produces exhilarating comic effects leading to a happy ending. Jojo undergoes an evolution and eventually frees Elsa. In the final scene of the film they both dance in the streets on the notes of David Bowie's song "We can be heroes, just for one day". Indeed, they are heroes: they have evolved and survived. In the book, conversely, it does not lead to a true emancipation of the protagonist that remains forever paralysed and trapped, this time in a new paranoia, where he re-configures himself as a hero only by subduing Elsa to his fantasies.

In conclusion, in the passage from page to screen the director Waititi has made cuts and additions. He has chosen to privilege the historical message of the book over the psychological relationship of the two main characters, emphasizing the effects of Nazi brainwashing on the younger population through para-military educational bodies such as *Hitlerjugend*, and he succeeds in showing its grotesque and paradoxical side. The invention of Hitler as an imaginary friend reinforces both the idea of the child's manipulated personality and the comical mode. The rise of the protagonist's awareness occurs not only thanks to historical and biographical facts, but also through his confrontation with the "other": his Jewish enemy, Elsa. Waititi includes Jojo's clumsy attempt to prevent Elsa from leaving the house, by lying on the winner of the war. However, the morbid love relationship that is developed in the book is soon avoided by the protagonist's reconsideration.

Although scientific criteria for assessing adaptations do not exist, *Jojo Rabbit* offers a truthful reconstruction of the historical context, provides the most important thread of the primary source, and conveys it from an original comical perspective. It is a good example of adaptation as a translation of a verbal text into another one, which uses a different medium. The changes adopted by Waititi, however, make it a new text which stands on its own: a side of the pyramid, in André Bazin's terms, and the result of intertextual dialogism, in Robert Stam's view. More simply, it is a skilfully directed movie constructed around a well-devised idea, which granted Taika Waititi an Academy Award for Best Adapted Screenplay in 2020.

Works Cited

Bazin, André: 'Adaptation, or the Cinema as Digest', in James Naremore (ed.): Film Adaptation. Rutgers University Press, New Brunswick 2014 [1948], pp. 19–27.
Bluestone, George: *Novels into Film*. Johns Hopkins Press, Baltimore 1957.
Cartmell, Deborah / Imelda Wheleha: *Screen Adaptation: Impure Cinema*. Palgrave Macmillan, London 2010.
Friedman, Ken / Diaz, Lily: 'Intermedia, Multimedia and Media', in: Diaz, Lily / Magda Dragu / Leena Eilittä (eds.): Adaptation and Convergence of Media. Aalto ARTS Books, Aalto University – School of Arts, Design and Architecture – Department of Media, Espoo, Finland 2018, pp. 26–60.
Kuryaev, I. / Osmukhina O.: 'Literature and Cinema: Aspects of Interaction', in: JOURNAL OF HISTORY CULTURE AND ART RESEARCH 2018/7, 3, pp. 376–383.
Leunens, Christine: Caging Skies. The Overlook Press, New York 2019.

Menon, Anil: 'Johannes in his burrow: Reading Christine Leunens' *Caging Skies*' in: THE HINDU May 30, 2020; available at: https://www.thehindu.com/books/johannes-in-his-burrow-christine-leunens-caging-skies-reviewed-by-anil-menon/article31708560.ece [accessed 12/6/2023].

Naremore, James: 'Film and the Reign of Adaptation', in: *Distinguished Lecture Series* 10, Institute and Society for Advanced Study, Distinguished lecture given on September 24, 1999, Indiana University, 1999.

Stam, Robert: 'Beyond Fidelity: The Dialogics of Adaptation', in: James Naremore (ed.): *Film Adaptation: An Anthology*. Rutgers Depth of Field Series, New Jersey 2000, pp. 54–76.

Waititi, Taika: *Jojo Rabbit*. 108 m. Fox Searchlight Pictures /TSG Entertainment (New Zealand, USA, Czech Republic 2019).

Zinnatullina et al in 2019: 'Literature and Cinema: Ways of Interaction in the 21ST Century', in: JOURNAL OF SOCIAL STUDIES EDUCATION RESEARCH 2019/10, 4, pp. 357–369.

Chiara Polli (University of Messina)

Graphic Reportage across Languages and Cultures. A Translational Perspective on Zerocalcare's Comics

Graphic Reportage: An Introduction

Although comics have often been associated with fiction and fun, ever since its early manifestations on the pages of US newspapers (e.g, Yellow Kid and its satire of New York society and sordid life in the slums), this medium has been strongly connected to the portrayal (and often satirical critique) of reality. Starting from late 1960s, US underground comix authors (Robert Crumb, Aline Kominsky, Justin Green, Art Spiegelman, among others) actually started to explore how comics could be a platform for autobiographical representations as well as for the expression of unfiltered personal opinions. According to Walker (2010), it is from this underground autobiographical tradition that much of today's graphic reportages emerge.

Graphic reportage or comic journalism – a term coined by one of its most prominent practitioners, Joe Sacco – can be defined as "serious non-fiction comics about current events" (Williams 2005, p. 52). Graphic reportage usually involves some sort of displacement: the events narrated take place far from the authors' comfort-zone and the journey to unfamiliar places is an integral part of the narration. Schlichting and Schmid (2019; n.p.) listed a number of features shared by the majority of graphic reportages: the focus on "traumatizing catastrophes" (e.g., war and oppression, displacement, natural disasters); the role of the authors as witnesses, whose accounts are "measured and filtered through [...] personal experiences" and "serve to reconstruct crises that tend to be overlooked in the mainstream media", thus positioning graphic non-fiction "as a distinct contemporary critique of dominant cultural norms of fact-finding and reportage". The asserted subjectivity of graphic narratives, in which the author-reporter "ostensibly takes liberties in interpreting actuality" (Schlichting and Schmid 2019, n.p.), openly breaks with reportage conventions and deconstructs the myth of the journalist's neutrality (Leveque 2010): often featuring themselves as characters and narrators, authors recount events by sharing personal feelings and interpretations of the events narrated. In graphic reportages, self-representation is not just a means to talk about the author's life, but becomes a device to plunge into a journey of stepwise discovery which involves getting in touch with other cultures and realities and ultimately aims to "materialize the experiences of *others*, often from marginalized groups" (Schlichting and Schmid 2019, n.p.). Through the gaze of the authors, readers can thus share their intercultural experience and develop empathic connections with the people and stories collected throughout the journey.

In light of all these considerations, this paper explores graphic reportage and its characteristics from a translational point of view. It focuses, in particular, on the English translation of one of the most celebrated Italian graphic reportages, Zerocalcare's *Kobane Calling* (KC henceforth) The aim of this study is to evaluate whether and how the process of translation – and thus of transfer to another language and culture – may affect the specificities of this genre (e.g., self-representation and subjectivity, combined intercultural dimension and critique to dominant cultural norms). To do so, Section 2 introduces the case-study and some theoretical premises, while Section 3 presents the results of a qualitative analysis of KC's English translation in comparison with the original. Finally, Section 4 provides some conclusive remarks, encouraging further research in this field.

Framing the 'Zerocalcare-phenomenon'

On 22 November 2020, the cover of the Italian weekly cultural magazine L'Espresso, titled: "L'ultimo Intellettuale" (The Last Intellectual) and presented Zerocalcare as a radical, desecrating and self-mocking comic author who has become the most influential storyteller of his generation. Zerocalcare, stage name of the Roman cartoonist Michele Rech, truly represents a unique editorial phenomenon in Italy. The 'Zerocalcare phenomenon' took the lead within the Italian underground scene, with which the author still maintains a strong connection, and then evolved thanks to the Internet with a blog[1] and the partnership with the publisher Bao, which published all of Zerocalcare's work starting from *La profezia dell'armadillo – Colore 8 bit* in 2012.[2] Zerocalcare's fame led him to break the boundaries of the so-called *ninth art*: for instance, the film version of *La profezia dell'armadillo* was presented at the Venice Film Festival in 2018, two art exhibitions were dedicated to Zerocalcare's art, i.e., *Scavare fossati – Nutrire Coccodrilli* (literally, "Digging Ditches-Nourishing Crocodiles") at the Museo Nazionale delle Arti del XXI Secolo in Rome between November 2018 and March

---

1 See www.zerocalcare.it [accessed 22/07/2023].
2 A first edition of the volume was self-published in 2011.

2019 (see Zerocalcare 2018) and *Zerocalcare. Dopo il Botto* at the Fabbrica del Vapore in Milan between December 2022 and April 2023 (see Zerocalcare 2023), and two animated series were written and directed by the author in collaborations with Netflix, i. e., *Strappare Lungo I Bordi* (2021; in English *Tear Along the Dotted Line*) and *Questo mondo non mi renderà cattivo* (2023; in English *This World Can't Tear Me Down*).

The key to Zerocalcare's success is mixing (self-)irony, surreal dialogues with his own conscience (with the features of an armadillo) and pop references in narratives that "evocano luoghi e sentimenti comuni, come l'incertezza di vivere in un mondo dove le disugualianze sociali sociali si fanno evidenti, la lotta per i diritti è debole e la ricerca di un lavoro sempre più difficile" ("evoke common places and feelings, such as the uncertainty of living in a world where social inequalities become evident, the fight for rights is weak and the job hunting is increasingly difficult"; Ferracci, 2018, p. 10). Zerocalcare's comics are defined "controstorie" ("counter-stories"; Melandri 2018, p. 4) and a "contro-storia d'Italia" (Barbagallo 2018, p. 6) because, while recounting his own personal experiences, the cartoonist in fact explores the civil drifts, social degradation, generational crisis and tragic events of the country (e. g. the G8 in Genoa in 2001) that have not entered the history books but which erode the foundations of Italian society. While maintaining its radical and strictly anti-fascist position, Zerocalcare still manages to speak to everyone – with a simple and fine language steeped in Roman-dialect traits – and interpret with sarcasm and great depth to the feelings of his generation.

However, KC, Zerocalcare's greatest international success, takes place far from the familiarity of his Roman neighbourhood, Rebibbia, the setting of most of his comics. KC is a reportage of the author's two journeys (in November 2014 and July 2015) to the Turkish-Syrian border, a few kilometres from the besieged town of Kobane, the symbol of the fight between Kurdish defenders of Rojava (YPG and YPJ) and the forces of the Islamic State.[3] Initially published as a short story in the magazine *Internazionale* in January 2015, KC was subsequently developed as a more ambitious and full-bodied project, which has become one of Italy's bestselling graphic novels (the fifth updated reprint, entitled *Kobane Calling. Oggi*, was published in 2020).[4]

KC was also translated into 10 languages (Basque, Czech, French, Japanese, Greek, English, Norwegian, Portuguese, Spanish, German). This is a countertrend in the Italian comics publishing industry. Italy is in fact considered an importer

---

3 In 2022, Zerocalcare published a second graphic reportage, *No Sleep till Shengal*, which covers another journey to the North of Iraq. Since the graphic novel has not been translated into English at the moment of writing this paper, it was excluded from the present analysis.
4 KC also received a theatrical transposition, adapted and directed by Nicola Zavagli and taken on tour in Italy during the 2019–20 theatre season.

of comics (Zanettin 2008; D'Arcangelo and Zanettin 2004; Rota 2003; Kaidl 1999). In particular, Rota (2003, p. 155) estimated that 70% of the comics published in Italy are translations; of these, 40% are US comics. With the exception of great masters such as Milo Manara, Guido Crepax, Hugo Pratt and some translations by Disney Italia and Bonelli, few Italian comics have succeeded in the opposite operation, i.e. to impose themselves on the US market. In 2017, the rights to KC were acquired by Magnetic Press, a publishing house that has been part of the US Lion Forge group since 2016. As underlined by the motto 'Comics for Everyone', Lion Forge sees itself as a comics publisher attentive to cultural diversity. The Magnetic collection, in particular, collects and translates the most successful international works into English. In the case of Zerocalcare, Magnetic chose to translate the complete version of KC, with the addition of "Groviglio" ("A Tangled Web"), a 12-page story taking stock of the events of the Turkish-Syrian conflict, published by the newspaper *Repubblica* in December 2012. The title given to the work is *Kobane Calling. Greetings from Northern Syria*, thus adding a geographical information about the setting of the reportage.

Through the analysis of KC's English version in comparison with the original, this article explores the complexities involved in the translation of a reportage which abounds of culture-bound references and linguistic traits that uniquely characterise the self-representation of the author and his characters.

These specificities may be particularly affected by translation. According to Venuti (1995/2008), there is a tendency, especially in contemporary Anglo-American publishing industry, to seek the so-called invisibility of the translator: translations aspire to be fluent and easily readable and the translator tends to opt for a domesticating strategy, which entails the ethnocentric reduction of the source text to the values of the target culture (p. 15), minimising foreign and unknown elements in favour of a reassuring reading. In contrast, Venuti identifies an foreignising approach to the text (pp. 15–16), which enhances the source text, protects its diversity, and do not bend it to the dominant target culture. It is therefore a matter of preserving the cultural identity of the foreign text through the translation process, accompanying the audience in a new – difficult but certainly enriching reading experience. In the case of comics, a medium in which the Anglo-American tradition is certainly dominant, there is a risk of losing the cultural specificity of products such as Zerocalcare's graphic reportage in favour of a domesticating translation which adapts the 'foreign' elements of the source materials to the target audience. Given the multimodal nature of comics (Kaindl 1999, 2004; Celotti 2008), the translation and possible domestication of these works do not involve only linguistic elements (captions, titles, balloons, paratextual elements), but also visual and typographic ones (images, colours, lines, format, lettering). In this respect, the present discussion takes into account how translation may affect meaning-making processes originating from the presence and interplay of different semiotic resources.

Kobane Calling in Translation

The present analysis is based on a qualitative investigation of KC's English version in comparison with the Italian original to pinpoint which strategies are adopted in the translation of this graphic reportage. In particular, in light of the considerations made in Section 1 and Section 2, three (potentially challenging) areas of interest are covered: 1. changes on a graphic and paratextual level; 2. the translation of language specificities; 3. the translation of culture-bound and autobiographical references. It should be noted that in a cartoon displaying the fictional "Carta dell'autogoverno di Rebibbia" (p. 246) ("Rebibbia self-government chart"), the English text is superimposed on an earlier German version. This may indicate the English translation is not based on the original Italian materials, but on the German ones (the German edition was published by Avant Verlag in 2017, some months before the English edition). Although there is no further data in this regard, the following considerations must therefore be read in the light of a possible mediation of the German language (and culture).

a)   Changes on a graphic and paratextual level

As for visual materials, the English version of KC do not present changes or deletions in the panels' images. However, some modifications occur in in terms of lettering. The English version attempts to digitally reproduce the original Italian freehand lettering: uppercase letters are used in captions and balloons when characters speak in Italian, italics when the characters speak in English, lower case in paratexts (e.g. mobile phone messages and newspaper excerpts). Nonetheless, the switch to English digital lettering entails a typographical standardisation, which is problematic for several reasons. In the original, font size and spacing perform several functions related to speech modulation: for instance, they mark the transition to higher tones of voice, indicate screams as well as Zerocalcare's alter-ego characteristic speech traits (e.g., he starts speaking quickly, without breathing as a manifestation of his anxiety). In this respect, the role of lettering is related to the visualisation of states of mind (no less than gaze, gesture, and facial expressions) and its standardisation determines a loss in terms of meaning. Furthermore, handwriting further personalises the narration by helping to recreate the illusion of reading the author's authentic travel diary – a feature that is lost in translation.

In the Italian version, the desire to recreate a sort of travel diary is announced in the subtitle included in the book's eyelet: "Facce, parole, scarabocchi da Rebibbia al confine turcosiriano" ("Faces, words, scribbles from Rebibbia to the Turkish-Syrian border"). With this sentence, Zerocalcare briefly summarises the essence of KC as a reportage that collects 'scribbles' of the thoughts, dialogues, experiences and people encountered during the journeys that took the author out of his own comfort zone, to reach Rojava, at the border between Turkey and Syria, where every day the battle to defend a model of democratic confederalism based on gender equality, environmental sustainability, religious and cultural pluralism is fought. However, in the English version this subtitle is not including, thus losing a first important element to frame the narration.

Likewise, at the beginning and end of the volume, Zerocalcare added two maps of the Kurdish territory and the Isis expansion between Syria and Iraq over in the time-span between the author's two journeys. The two maps are reproduced in English, but some paratextual elements are missing: in particular, in the first map, the handwritten reference to the final one is removed ("Nei risguardi finali c'è la mappa del secondo viaggio"; "In the end-paper there is the map of the second journey"). In the original, this note increases the 'scribbled' style of the volume, which is characterised from the outset by the high number of notes and annotations. This is a device which may actually facilitate the task of the translator who, as we shall see, is free to add notes and explanations without the space limitations usually imposed in comics, while maintaining a certain coherence with the free and 'scribbled' style of the author. Similar to lettering, the choice to use notes contribute to the aforementioned illusory effect of reading a travel diary, written on the spur of the moment, confidential and informal in register and style. In the same map, all the colloquiality and spontaneity of Zerocalcare's style emerges in notes such as the one describing Kobane: "Coatto 'sto puntino bianco circondato da Isis, eh?". In English, the specificity of the regionalism "coatto" (that here refers ironically to the arrogance of the little town of Kobane, which still resists despite being surrounded by the Islamic State) as well as the informal register is lost with the more neutral: "Impressive, this little white dot surrounded by Daesh, no?".

This brief example highlights two criticalities which Zerocalcare's translator has to deal with: i) the presence of regionalisms and, in particular, terms typical of the Roman dialect which convey unique and hardly replicable semantic nuances, most of which are clearly comprehensible to the entire Italian audience but difficult to render in other languages; ii) the continuous clash between formal and informal registers that contribute to creating the tension between comic and dramatic, between lightness and seriousness that characterises Zerocalcare's narration both verbally and graphically.

b)   The translation of language specificities

The challenge in translating Zerocalcare's language is that his style mixes colloquialisms and expression typical of youth slang, drug culture, neologisms and regionalisms, which are hard to reproduce.

The Roman dialect is spoken by almost every character in Zerocalcare's world, ironically even by characters who are not from Rome (e. g., the Kurds on pp. 157 and 175). The author fully exploits the 'colorful' nature of the Roman dialect as a comic device, by playing with its phonetic and grammatical characteristics (elisions, consonantal doublings, the use of the verb "stare" instead of "essere", the mutation of /ʎ/ into [j], rotacism phenomena, the inversion between possessive adjective and noun, among others) as well as with a set of creative and bizarre expressions, with great communicative value even for those who are not familiar with the dialect (though, as stressed below, sometimes the author himself adds notes and explanations on the emphatic value of these terms).

A number of key-terms and phrases from the Roman dialect have become part of the idiolect of Zerocalcare's comic alter-ego. Among the expressions that have become part of what we may call Zerocalcare's glossary, the only expression translated with a certain consistency by using the same equally colloquial solution is the slur "porcoddue", which is rendered with "for pork's sake". As the following examples will detail, however, the other terms are not preserved consistently and their comical as well as identitarian value is largely lost.

Among the most famous expressions used by Zerocalcare, we have "daje" (or "daje forte") and "li mortacci tua", often abbreviated to the forms "mortacci tua" and "tacci tua". In KC, the authors dedicates two notes to both terms. As for the former, he comments: "(Daje va proprio bene per ogni situazione. Meno male che sono romano, oh.)" (literally, "(Daje is good in every situation. Good thing I am Roman, oh.)", p. 19). The English version takes advantage of the note to clarify the meaning of the term and, thus, preserve the regionalism: "(Since 'daje' means everything from 'no way' to 'come on' it always applies. Good thing I'm from Rome cause they don't use it anywhere else)". In this case, the translator opts to add an explanation of the term in the note.

As for "limortaccitua", Zerocalcare explains how: "(Sì, a Roma limortacci tua può essere uno sfregio o una carezza, dipende tutto sa chi lo dice, quando e con che inflessione.)" (literally, "Yes, in Rome, limortacci tua can be a slur or a caress, depending on who says it, when and with what inflection; p. 143). The English version maintains the expression in the title (though detaching the words that in the original are joined) and in the balloon in which it is fist used. In the note, a fuller explanation of the term is added, with information that would not be required for an Italian reader of Zerocalcare but are required to orient the target audience of the translation: "(So this is a typical Roman slang term that basically means 'your bad dead ancestors', but it can be offensive or affectionate, depending on who says it, when, and with what tone.)".

In these two cases, the translator adopts a strategy translation strategy known as "amplification" (Malone, 1988), which is used to fill a linguistic-cultural gap (in this case to clarify the dialectal expressions) whose presence has an foreignising effect for English-speaking readers. Despite the explanatory notes and the evident communicative value of Zerocalcare's idioms, however, the expressions "daje" and "mortaccitua" are not maintained in Italian throughout the volume.

The term "daje" is translated with colloquial but certainly less colourful solutions such as "come on" (p. 62), "cool" (p. 133), or a generic "good job" (p. 155). The different variants of "li mortacci tua" are translated with "omifuckinggod!" (p. 13), "you bastards" (p. 59) or "screw you guys" (p. 209). On page 25, in the original caption "Checcazzoteridi, 'tacci tua" (literally, "why are you fucking laughing, 'tacci tua") is modified as: "Oh yeah, fucking hilarious", thus omitting the Roman phrase.

In both cases, not only the translator decides not to preserve the original key-terms (taking advantage of the explanatory notes), but their translation also lack of consistency as no unique solution is adopted to translate the terms. In so doing, two recurring linguistic elements characterising Zerocalcare's speech are erased and his idiolect is impoverished. Likewise, other recurring Roman expressions such as "avoja" (translated as "totally", p. 60) and "sticazzi" (translated as "whatever", p. 61) are normalised using terms that raise the communicative register and are inappropriate to the situation. Eliminating the slang of the characters determines a loss in the comedic effect generated by the clash between the seriousness of the themes and events narrated and the light-hearted spontaneous personality of the characters that experience and narrate them.

Language standardisation causes a loss in the way in which some of Zerocalcare's friends are characterised. For example, in the English version, the character of Gabriele (adapted into Gabriel), who briefly appears to accompany the author for part of the second journey, is less crude, blunt and vulgar than in the original comics. The normalisation of his speech is evident from this short example: the sentence "Rega', io ve lo dico, mi accollo a voi solo per il viaggio fino a Erbil perchè ci abita la pischella mia limortaccisua" is translated as: "Guys, I'm telling you, I'm coming along just for the trip to Erbil. My girlfriend lives there." The overall meaning of the sentence is the same, but the elimination of the regionalisms "regà", "accollo", "pischella mia" and "limortaccisua", the use of neutral language and a higher register largely modify character in the eyes of the readers as he no longer appears the same coarse, tough guy of the originals. Among these words, the term "accollo" (and the verb "accollarsi", in this case rendered with a neutral "coming along") deserves a particular mention as another key-word in Zerocalcare's glossary (one of his volumes is entitled *L'elenco telefonico degli accolli*, literally "The nuisances' phone book" 2015) whose use has now become popular among young people far beyond the borders of Rome.

In Roman dialect, "accollo" indicates, in a figured sense, nagging, annoying and pedantic people, but also the set of responsibilities and commitments undertaken and, in the case of Zerocalcare, the countless eclectic commissions and requests that he is incessantly facing. In a word, "accollo" encompasses all nuisances. The recurring use of the term Zerocalcare's alter-ego is a comic device which acts as a sort of trademark, making him recognisable, and contributing to characterising his personality as a figure constantly torn between a sense of guilt and the need to escape from some sort of nuisance.

The English translation of KC does not consider the importance of this word and the translator neither preserves it nor attempts to find an equivalent to use consistently so as to uniquely characterise the character's speech. In many cases, the translation reduces the meaning of the term to a precise type of job-related "accollo": "work" (p. 47), "obligations" (p. 48), "deadlines" (p. 52), and "chores" (p. 98). In addition to erasing an identitarian element of Zerocalcare's alter-ego, the semantic reference to annoying people is missing and, to some extent, the strongly negative connotation of the term is weakened. Furthermore, these lexical choices neutralise the text and raise its register.

In a few cases, the translation misrepresents the meaning of the verb "accollarsi", as the following examples show:

A) Original: Che poi so' vecchi e bambini strani, non s'accollano, non ti fanno domande, non ti dicono "Cannavaro!" e non ti chiedono se sei del Milan o della Juve. Ti fissano e basta. (p.36) [literally, "Plus, old people and children are strange, they don't *cling* (*accollarsi*), they don't ask you questions, they don't say 'Cannavaro!' to you and they don't ask you if you root for Milan or Juve. They just stare at you."].

Translation: Plus old people and children are strange, they have no responsibilities, they don't ask you anything, they don't mistake you for Cannavaro or ask you what football team you root for. They just stare at you.

B) Original: Scusa, ma non ho capito…Ma Nasrin se li accolla tutti? (p. 150) [literally, "Sorry, but I didn't understand…But Nasrin *takes them all on* ("*se li accolla*")?]

Translation: Sorry, I don't understand…Does Nasrin train all of them?

In the first case, the original text wants to emphasise the composure of the children and elderly of the Rojava refugee camp who strangely do not bother and annoy the protagonist, little inclined to social interactions and openly anxious in front of these two categories. Conversely, the translation "they have no responsibilities" seems to emphasise, incorrectly, how children and the elderly are carefree categories. Unlike the original, the translation seems to oppose these two categories without responsibilities to those who actually have responsibility, i.e., the people who remained in Kobane to fight (mentioned in the subsequent panels).

It is interesting to note that in the same example, the translation eliminates the explicit references to the Italian football teams AC Milan and Juventus FC, preferring the generalisation "football teams". By contrast, the reference to the popular Italian footballer Fabio Cannavaro is kept, although in the original it is not made explicit that the protagonist is mistaken for Cannavaro.

In the subsequent examples, "accollarsi" is incorrectly rendered as "train", thus making reference to the fact that Commander Nasrin, head of the Rojava Women's Protection Units (the YPJ), trained many of the fighters who fell in the field. In fact, the original refers to how Nasrin reserved care and attention to the families of the fallen fighters, taking care of all of them. The original, rather than referring to training activities, is emphasising the strength and empathy of Commander Nasrin, who is carry the weight of the conflict consequences (i.e., the death of her comrades) on her shoulders. This a touching moment of the story that – as frequently occurs in Zerocalcare's comics – is filtered by the use of dialects to convey spontaneity and create a bittersweet clash between the down-to-earth attitude of the protagonist and the tragic nature of what he is witnessing.

From these examples, it is evident how, the absence of a single, coherent term to translate 'accollo' and 'accollarsi' generates a loss in the characterisation of the protagonist through his idiolect. In addition, the translation often falls into error, completely changing the original meaning of the original text.

Another example of neutralised colloquial/dialectal register is the rendering of the Roman word "pippone"' another key word in Zerocalcare's glossary used with a clear comical connotation in the case of boring explanations or long, serious and detailed speeches. In the case of KC, Zerocalcare uses a lot of "pipponi" to add details, notes, and maps that can inform readers who are not familiar with the situation in Rojava. At the same, the people Zerocalcare meets often "attaccano pipponi" or "attaccano 'na pippa", when they dwell on speeches deemed too heavy by the protagonist. In this case, the dialect expression is normalised using "lecture" (e.g., pp. 8, 9, 19, 53, 54, 76, 204), a term which neutralises the semantic charge and comical value of the original and elevates the register. The same register mistake is to be noted when, instead of "pippone", Zerocalcare uses the synonym "riassuntone" (p. 204), a colloquial form of "riassunto" ("summary") formed with the augmentative, which in translation becomes "synopsis". Overall, by using these neutralising strategies, the translation of the volume elevates the register of the original and, in the English version, the clash between the Roman spirit (and its down-to-earth, light-hearted, and comical connotation) and the world of war and sacrifice of Rojava is less strong, almost absent.

c) The translation of culture-bound and autobiographical references

The author's comedy often relies on cultural references which are comprehensible only to readers with a certain degree of familiarity with Italy. In addition, Zerocalcare's texts are also imbued with links to the reality of the social centres, activism, demonstrations, occupations, anti-fascism and far-left political militancy.

Translating this web of references is a complex and delicate challenge. In KC, some cultural references have been rendered with a generalisation: the toponym Rimini becomes a generic "riviera" (p. 99), although most toponyms are faithfully maintained; the reference to the Anonima Sequestri sarda is replaced by "Sardinian bandits" (p. 215); the "partigiana romana Carla Capponi" becomes "Italian partisan" (p. 227). In the balloon: "Allora è tutta una merda e siamo meglio noi con Belpietro, Libero, Pigibattista e il Gabibbo." (p. 175), the proper names of journalists, the extreme right-wing newspaper Libero and the TV mascot Gabibbo are rendered with the generalisation: "talking heads and news mascots", losing the obvious negative connotation that the original referents have. In one case, "media italiani" are adapted to "western media" (p. 10).

As in the case of AC Milan and Juventus FC seen above, in the balloon "Se proprio ti dice male finisci a chiedere informazioni al bar dei laziali, tiè" (p. 80), the reference to the fans of SS Lazio football team ("bar dei laziali") is generalised in: "Really bad luck and you ask directions at the wrong team's bar, ha!". In Italian, the reference implies a set of shared knowledge between Zerocalcare and his readers: first, the fact that the cartoonist sympathises with the rival team of SS Lazio, AC Roma; second, the well-known right-wing extremism of several SS Lazio supporters. Both in terms of football affiliation and political ideas, Zerocalcare stands at the opposite of SS Lazio's fans and therefore a step into the wrong bar would certainly 'mean troubles'. While, for an Italian reader, especially one already familiar with the author's stories, this inference is immediate, the English target readers may struggle to understand the cultural reference behind the cartoon. For this reason, the translation opts for a far more familiar generalization regarding "wrong teams".

One of KC's recurring moments of comedy is Zerocalcare's gastronomic culture clash as he steps out of his comfort zone of snacks, industrial products, and Roman food to discover Middle Eastern culinary traditions. In cases of references to typical Roman dishes, "amatriciana" is kept unchanged, but "guanciale" is replaced by a more familiar "pancetta"; "cacioeppepe" is rendered "cacio e pepe". In this case, the original spelling aimed to mimic the consonantal doubling typical of the Roman dialect and composes a neologism "cacioeppepe" to unambiguously identify the traditional dish (p. 142).

Zerocalcare's character is also famous for his addiction to plumcakes, which is the theme of recurring comic sketches in all his works. In KC, the English version ignores the centrality of plumcakes as a recurring comical element, translating the term with a generic "snack cake" (p. 18). Even the other snacks desired by the protagonist, in the absence of plumcakes, (e.g., Kinder Brioss, Camilla alle carote, briciole di Pandistelle) are rendered with as many generic terms ("kinder bar", "slice of carrot bread", "biscuit crumbs"). In contrast, the English version omits the brief explanation of what chai is ("una specie di tè"; "a kind of tea") present in the original caption. Chai will become the protagonist's new addiction and therefore the author adds an explanation for Italian readers unfamiliar with this product, which however is deemed superfluous for the translator.

In another case, when the original makes a generic reference to a US cultural product such as the Muppets ("io accanto a lei sembro la rana dei Muppets"; literally, "next to her, I look like the frog from the Muppets"), the English version opts for a specification of the reference: "She [...] makes me seem like Kermit the frog" (p. 34).

Zerocalcare's comics also abounds with references to cinema, TV series and cartoons. For example, in KC, he compares a political activist he met in Iraq to "ingegner Filini" (p.105), a cinematographic character played in the comic film saga *Fantozzi* (1975–1999) by Gigi Reder. In the films, Filini is the friend and colleague of the protagonist. He is semi-blind, very precise and zealous in his work but equally submissive and bullied by the bosses. The comical nature of this reference lies in the contrast between the meek appearance of the character encountered by Zerocalcare and his actual story, characterise by courage, militancy, torture, and suffering, worth of a film like *Die Hard*, as the author stresses in a subsequent passage. In English, given the missing cultural references to *Fantozzi*, the translator opted for a generic "seems like some boring old accountant." While trying to preserve a link with Filini's character, the generalisation causes a loss from the point of view of semantic connotations, since Filini is not only the symbol of boredom and pedantry, but also of submissiveness and ridiculousness. Furthermore, with this generalisation the contrast between the comedy film (*Fantozzi*) and the action film (*Die Hard*), which contributes to the general comical effect of the panel, is erased.

Another missing reference to Italian cinema regards *Amici Miei* by Mario Monicelli (1975) on page 110, where Zerocalcare ironically translates his friend Ezel's speech as: "Traduzione un po' approssimativa: 'Senza contare la supercazzola prematurata come fosse Antani, no?'" The original takes up the nonsense neologisms coined in the film (i.e., "supercazzola prematurata come fosse Antani"), whose dialogues are an emblem of speech devoid of logical sense but apparently polished, exploiting concatenations of high-sounding but non-existent words in order to confuse and even persuade the disoriented interlocutors.

The English translation of this passage is: "Loose translation: 'Without considering the brillig and the slithy toves, right?'". In this case, the translator retrieves the reference to the "Jabberwocky", the nonsense poem found in *Through the Looking-Glass* (1871) by Lewis Carroll. The adaptation in this case sacrifices the film reference to try to preserve the original nonsense and the idea that Ezel is trying to beguile a guard at the border to obtain permission to go to Rojava.

In this and other cases, the translator opted for a cultural adaptation, thus domesticating the source text to make it intelligible to the English-speaking reader. Other instances are the Italian news programme Studio Aperto, which becomes CNN (p. 79); the chain of chain of electronics shops Media World, which become Best Buy (p. 107), the Italian theme song of the Japanese anime *Occhi di Gatto* (originally *Cat's Eye*), which becomes that of the cartoon Scooby-Boo (p. 135), the underwear shop chain Tezenis, which becomes TJ Maxx (p. 156). In one only one case, the reference to the Standa chain of shops is deleted (p. 13).

On some occasions, the translator opts to leave foreignising references by adding explanations and notes or by amplifying the text. As mentioned, these solutions suit Zerocalcare's style, which frequently uses footnotes, arrows and asterisks and leaves abundant space for additions, without graphically modifying the images, captions or balloons. For instance, in the passage where Zerocalcare quotes the verses of the Italian singer Max Pezzali (p. 30), the English version amplifies the text: "There's this singer Max Pezzali..."; similarly, the reference to the cartoonist Gipi is maintained, adding a note at the bottom of the page with the explanation "Italian cartoonist Gianni Pacinotti" (p. 120); the reference to Barbapapà, the protagonist of the children's book series of the same name created by Annette Tisot and Talus Taylor, is amplified by adding "very popular and comforting children's character" (p. 154); when Zerocalcare refers to the lira and in a footnote explains how the Italian expression Italian "non caccia una lira" is "corretta e non vintage" since the lira still exists in Turkey, the English version adds the explanation "correct and not vintage pre-euro" (p. 34), amplifying the text to clarify the cultural reference and the comicality derived from the pun to the old Italian currency to English-speaking readers.

The quotation from Carlo Verdone's film *Bianco, rosso e Verdone* (1981) is translated from the Roman into English: "This hand can be hard as iron, or soft as silk" ("sta mano po' esse fero e po' esse piuma."), adding the references to the actor who pronounces it in the film, Mario Brega, and to the film. The translation is clearly amplified, explaining the terms of comparison and normalising the language, but still tries to preserve the foreign element (though the inevitable loss of the dialect diminishes the communicative charge of the sentence, which for a *connoisseur* of the film takes on a special value being placed in the context of the Kurds' struggles against Isis).

Zerocalcare often makes extensive use of songs combined with his drawings. In the case of KC, two songs close the two parts of the story: "L'oltretorrente" (pp. 43–45) and "La preghiera dei banditi" (pp. 248–250) by Atarassia Gröp. In the first case, the English translation shows the original title (as chapter title and as a paratext, in the mp3 player of the protagonist). In the second case, the song title is translated when it coincides with the chapter title, but an explanatory note is added: "Lyrics from 'La preghiera dei banditi', an anti-war song by Italian band Atarassia Gröp". In both cases, the verses are not left Italian but translated.

In some cases, the translation leaves references to Italian characters without explanations (e.g. Gianni Morandi on page 27, and Aldo Moro on page 66), perhaps because no annotation was considered necessary. A particular example is found on page 212, where Zerocalcare refers to the Italian television programme Forum, in which each episode features often fictitious and exaggerated reconstructions of court cases. The English translation leaves a generic "the forum", i.e., the court. In this case, although the cultural reference is lost, the comical effect is maintained in the cartoon, which ironically depicts a farmer suing the PKK for stealing three apples from his tree.

As mentioned beforehand, Zerocalcare's translator is required to know how to translate adequately some key terms belonging to his political-cultural background and autobiographical experiences. In KC, this sometimes does not happen. For instance, it would have been essential to translate terms of political significance such as "compagno/comrade" (wrongly rendered as "they", p. 24), "borghese/bourgeois" (rendered as "classy" and thus deprived of the meaning linked to the class struggle, p. 49), the "Arci clubs" (wrongly translated "gym", p. 97), and "guerra partigiana/partisan war" (replaced by the explanation: "Italian Resistance in WWII", p. 202).

In a key passage of the journey, where Zerocalcare and his companions learn of the kamikaze attack on the Kurdish cultural centre of Amara in Turkish Kurdistan, the author draws a comparison with July 2001 tragic events of the G8 summit in Genoa, a key event in his life, which he witnessed directly: "mentre lo scrivo realizzo che lo stesso giorno, 14 anni prima, a Genova moriva Carlo Giuliani" (literally, "as I'm writing this, I realise that the same day, 14 years earlier, Carlo Giuliani died in Genoa", p. 95). For Zerocalcare's readers, it is obvious that this comparison implies the author's shock on learning the news of the attack on Amara. The English translation adds more information for readers who are unfamiliar with the G8: "As I'm writing this, I realise that this is the same day, fourteen years earlier, that Carlo Giuliani was killed protesting the G8 summit in Genoa". The addition is necessary because it is important that English audience understands the critical role of these events and how significant is this comparison for the author, although they are mentioned in this single passage and the symbolic value of Carlo Giuliani's death may still be obscure.

Another central element to fully understand Zerocalcare's comics is the reference to his neighbourhood, Rebibbia, to which the author is firmly attached, despite the stigma due to the presence of the prison of the same name, one of the largest in Italy. On page 107, the author describes the scene of people patiently waiting for days and days for permission to cross the border between Iraq and Syria to get to Rojava: "E negli occhi di tutti quelli che incontri, c'è una cosa familiare [...]. È una cosa che sta a Rebibbia. Che impari guardandoti intorno, nelle facce di tutta l'umanità che ruota attorno a quell'enorme deposito coatto di corpi che è il carcere. L'attesa." (literally, "And in the eyes of everyone you meet, there is something familiar [...]. It is something that is in Rebibbia. That you learn by looking around, in the faces of all humanity that revolves around the huge forced repository of bodies that is the prison. The waiting."). The translation of the passage is: "And in the eyes of everyone you meet, there's something familiar [...]. You can see it in Rebibbia, or at a prison. Something you learn by looking around, into the faces of all the humanity that gravitate around an in this massive cage. The waiting". The translation loses the reference to the prison of Rebibbia by using the disjunctive conjunction "or" and thus addressing a generic prison. In so doing, the English version does not convey the same sense of familiarity that the scene generates for the author, who perceives that the people waiting to pass the border share the same feelings that dominate Rebibbia's prison, thus connotatively associating them to prisoners and, at the same time, to people he understands and feels close to.

Conclusion

As a graphic reportage, KC is a narration of displacement, encounter with *otherness* and culture shock. It recounts the personal experience of the author at the Turkish-Syrian borders and, by reading a sort of 'scribble' notebook or diary, readers also experience the life, hopes and suffering of Rojava though Zerocalcare's eyes, his ideas, his system of thought and knowledge. The asserted subjectivity of this reportage is constantly reminded by the continuous autobiographical incursions, culture-bound references to the author's background as well as by the use of comical devices in which reality and facts are clearly manipulated for the sake of a more light-hearted humour (e.g., the Kurds using the Roman dialect). The task of translating this work is certainly challenging as it entails the translation of the author's idiolect as well as the re-creation of a universe of characters (above all, his alter-ego) which are strongly connoted by features that English readers may perceive as unintelligible, distant, foreign – and would thus require long explanations in order to be clarified.

In general, according to D'Arcangelo and Zanettin (2004, p. 197), given the tendency of US comics to favour short dialogues (less dense than Italian ones), comics translated into English often suffer from substantial cuts in order to reduce the source texts and 'tame' them to suit the taste of the English-speaking public, who privileges action and is not accustomed to long reading times. In some cases, the comparative analysis of the Italian and the English versions of KC revealed a first attempt to overcome the domesticating approach to translation and opening up to foreignizing elements by adopting a strategy of textual amplification with the aim of adding information for English-speaking readers, guiding them in the understanding of some of the cultural references in which the comic book is rich.

This attempt to embrace culturally different elements is appreciable, although it lacked of consistency and continuity. In general, the translation disregarded several key-concepts and words which belong to the idiolect and the autobiographical experience of the author, from the recurring use of dialectal terms, to political references to militancy and anti-fascism, until the microcosm revolving around Rebibbia and its prison. In this respect, in a number of cases, the translator opted for generalisations which ultimately narcotised some of the original's semantic references and connotations.

Furthermore, in the English version of KC there was no effective attempt to render of the linguistic specificities of Zerocalcare's work. Conversely, the translation normalised Zerocalcare's lexicon, elevated the communicative register and, in so doing, eliminated some linguistic peculiarities (e.g., the repetition of terms such as "daje" and "mortacci tua", which were explained in a note but never used from there onwards) that in the original contribute to characterise Zerocalcare's universe and its inhabitants. In translation, some comical devices were also missing (e.g., the clash between low register or pop culture references with tragedy): this affects the work's communicative power and fails to reproduce the peculiarity of Zerocalcare's style as one of his most appreciated skill lies in combining tragic elements (e.g. the Kurdish war against Isis) with comical elements (e.g. the desecrating Roman-spirit of the characters, shown off in a variety of contexts).

It is perhaps no coincidence that Zerocalcare's success abroad has been greater in countries such as France, where the translator is close to the author's political and cultural sensibility, and the works have been accompanied by glossaries to understand the Roman cartoonist's key-words. In this respect, further studies providing a comparative analysis of English and French translations are encouraged.

Despite the clear difficulty of translating KC, the choice to publish this complex and culture-bound work in English indicates a general openness to a foreignising approach and marks a clear change of course from the trend of the past. In this light, new studies should explore the specificities of graphic reportage and discuss this genre in relation to translation so as to gain new insights into its intercultural dimension and the stimulating challenges it provides to translators.

Works Cited

Barbagallo, S.: 'Faccio le cose perché le sento dentro, ma non le so spiegare', in Zerocalcare (ed.), *Scavare fossati nutrire coccodrilli*. Bao Publishing, Milan 2018, pp. 6-7.
Celotti, N.; 'The translator of Comics as a Semiotic Investigator', in: F. Zanettin (ed.), *Comics in Translation*. St Jerome Publishing, Manchester 2008, pp. 33-49.
D'Arcangelo, A. / Zanettin F.: 'Dylan Dog Goes to the USA: A North-American Translation of an Italian Comic Book Series', in: ACROSS LANGUAGES AND CULTURES, 2004/5 (2), pp. 187-211.
Ferracci, G.: 'Zerocalcare e il coraggio che non diserta la società civile', in: Zerocalcare (ed.), *Scavare fossati nutrire coccodrilli*. Bao Publishing, Milan 2018, pp. 10-12.
Kaindl, K.: 'Thump, Whizz, Poom: A Framework for the Study of Comics under Translation', in: TARGET, 1999/11 (2), pp. 263-88.
Kaindl, K.: 'Multimodality in the Translation of Humour in Comics', in: E. Ventola / C. Charles / M. Kaltenbacher (eds.), *Perspectives on Multimodality*. John Benjamins, Amsterdam and Philadelphia 2004, pp. 173-92.
L'Espresso. L'ultimo intellettuale (22 november 2020). *L'ESPRESSO* (cover).
Lévêque S. (2010). Introduction. In Lévêque S., Ruellan D., (Eds.), *Journalistes engagés* (pp. 9-16). Rennes: Presses Universitaires de Rennes.
Malone, J. L. (1988). *The science of linguistics in the art of translation: Some tools from linguistics for the analysis and practice of translation*. Albany, N.Y: State University of New York Press.
Melandri, G.: 'Prefazione', in: Zerocalcare (ed.), *Scavare fossati nutrire coccodrilli*. Bao Publishing, Milan 2018, p. 5.
Park, E. / Chute, H.: 'The Best Graphic Novels of 2020', 9 December 2020. Retrieved from: https://www.nytimes.com/2020/12/09/books/review/best-graphic-novels.html [Accessed: 21/02/2021]
Rota, V.: 'I fumetti. Traduzione e adattamento', in: TESTO A FRONTE 2003/28, pp. 155-172.
Schlichting, L. & Schmid, J.: 'Introduction to Graphic Realities: Comics as Documentary, History, and Journalism', in: IMAGETEXT, 2019/11 (1), n.p.
Venuti, L.: The Translator's Invisibility: A History of Translation. Routledge, London & New York 1995/2008.
Walker, T.: 'Graphic Wounds: The Comics Journalism of Joe Sacco', in: JOURNEYS 2010/11 (1), pp. 69-88.
Williams, K.: 'The Case for Comics Journalism', in: COLUMBIA JOURNALISM REVIEW March/April 2005, pp. 51-55.
Zanettin, F.: 'Comics in Translation: An Overview', in: F. Zanettin (ed.), *Comics in Translation*. St Jerome Publishing, Manchester 2008 pp. 1-32.
Zerocalcare: Kobane Calling, in: INTERNAZIONALE 16 January 2015, pp. 33-74.

Zerocalcare: La profezia dell'armadillo. Edizioni Graficart, Rome 2011.
Zerocalcare: La profezia dell'armadillo – Colore 8 bit. Bao Publishing, Milan 2012.
Zerocalcare: L'elenco telefonico degli accolli. Bao Publishing, Milan 2015.
Zerocalcare: Kobane Calling. Bao Publishing, Milan 2016.
Zerocalcare: 'Groviglio', in: La Repubblica 24 December 2016, p. 69.
Zerocalcare: Kobane Calling: Greetings from Northern Syria. Magnetic Press, Chicago 2017.
Zerocalcare: Kobane Calling. Oggi. Bao Publishing, Milan 2020.
Zerocalcare: No Sleep till Shengal. Bao Publishing, Milan 2022.

Maria Festa (University of Torino)

Crossing Borders with the "Refugee Tales" Project

Introduction

Literature has been defined by several critics as a continuous experiment in form, and indeed literature is in constant evolution, always reworking and transforming genres, motifs and conventions inherited from a past tradition (Landa 2007, p. 143). With Landa's thinking in mind, this paper takes into consideration interdisciplinary and transdisciplinary approaches to anglophone postcolonial literature. The last decades have witnessed the proliferation of new narrative modes such as weblogs, social media posts, video poems, digital publications and digital essayims. Besides weaving together multiple storytelling forms including fiction, testimony, (auto)biography, orality, performativity and visuality, these diversified narratives also allow to emphasise the persisting issues at the core of anglophone postcolonial literature, that is to say racism, identity, belonging, displacement and alienation. It is not by chance then that the digital world and new multimodal textual forms fostered by new media interact with this literary genre and most relevantly with migration and refugee narratives.

Furthermore, the concept of literature may also convey the idea of a point of convergence of different fields of research and episteme, a centre around which other disciplines revolve, meet and merge with. According to one of Caryl Phillips's definitions of literature, literature may represent for authors and readers both a medium "to know about people" (Phillips 2011, p. 111) and a means of "travelling furiously across borders and boundaries" (Phillips 2001, p. 5). Following from this, to some extent, it may be argued that the figurative passing through lines that separates one country from another feasible when dealing with a literary work may be understood as another kind of crossing, that is to say the act of crossing different disciplinary boundaries to create a holistic approach. Drawing knowledge from different fields of research allows founder members and authors behind the "Refugee Tales" project to deliver an elaborated and truthful account of events that are instead omitted, neglected or misinterpreted by mainstream narrative. In point of fact, brought forth and developed within the Gatwick Detainees Welfare group registered charity, the "Refugee Tales" project represents an explicit instance of interdisciplinary and transdisciplinary approaches to anglophone postcolonial literature. The "Refugee Tales" is a humanitarian, activist project that relies on individuals with heterogenous cultural background and knowledge who voluntarily cooperate employing in return a true synthesis of approaches to migration and refugee narratives. In doing so, the "Refugee Tales" project aims at shedding light on the issue of immigration detention in the United Kingdom simultaneously giving voice to those human beings who experienced hazardous journeys made in quest of better, dignified, just and unbiased life conditions only to arrive at Western immigration removal centres.

The "Refugee Tales" Project: how it started

The Gatwick Detainees Welfare Group (GDWG) was set up in 1995 in response to the UK Immigration Service as it began to detain people at a small holding centre near Gatwick Airport. This online organization instantly exhibited its militant, activist agency. It is a non-party organization that made itself known chiefly on the Internet whose well-designed website is a recipient that gathers practical and legal information for migrants and refugees, updated news, links to social media such as Facebook and Twitter, along with other helpful contact channels. The Gatwick Detainees Welfare Group's mission as clearly stated on its homepage "supporting people during and after detention" (https://www.gdwg.org.uk/) is to assist newly arrived migrants, refugee asylum seekers and those arrested for illegal staying in the United Kingdom. This registered charity is a project of humanitarian activism that reveals the entangled, and often impenetrable, links between language and culture that have created an inhumane immigration system in the United Kingdom or the former colonizer that identified itself as the 'mother country'.

In 2015, David Herd – poet, professor of modern literature, activist – and Anna Pincus – director of Gatwick Detainees Welfare Group – launched a wider campaign in defence of migrants' rights which is "an outreach project of Gatwick Detainees Welfare Group inspired by the experiences of men held in immigration detention at Gatwick and the work of the group in 20 years of visiting" (https://www.gdwg.org.uk/).

Herd and Pincus increased the Gatwick Detainees Welfare Group's commitment to support people affected by immigration detention and expanded the original website by adding a new link to a further project of humanitarian activism named "Refugee Tales", which draws on Geoffrey Chaucer's *The Canterbury Tales* (1387–1388) for inspiration. Since 2015, every summer through the

English countryside, "walks of solidarity", as defined by Herd (Herd 2016, p. 133), take place over several days of trekking and telling stories along the way. The storytelling that occurs during the event turns later into a collection of stories published by Comma Press, a not-for-profit, Manchester based publisher and development agency. So far Herd and Pincus have already edited four volumes titled *Refugee Tales* (2016, 2017, 2019, 2021). This additional form of activism that was brought to life on the Internet under a literary viewpoint originated a remarkable role reversal. It gives a platform and humanity to the often-voiceless Others, outsiders – the typical characters of postcolonial literature – who now have the chance to become the storytellers and/or authors of their own narratives, i.e. their life experiences. Their account of events, anecdotes or mere fragmented thoughts are told to volunteers who share values at the core of the "Refugee Tales" project and, among them, there are also well famous postcolonial writers such as Abdulrazak Gurnah (the winner of the Nobel Prize in Literature 2021), Ali Smith, Patience Agbabi, Jackie Kay, Kamila Shamsie, Monica Ali, Bernardine Evaristo along with intellectuals and activists such as Philippe Sands, Maurizio Veglio and many other relevant writers. These first-hand life experiences told by impromptu storytellers are later accurately written down, and on this occasion a pure collaborative, synergic relationship between the improvised teller and the celebrity writer takes place. The latter, that is to say the well-established and by now canonical postcolonial author momentarily sets aside her/his own writing style and the proper narrative techniques to let the teller's voice predominate on paper. In contrast to how the migrants are muted, or written out of legal and bureaucratic discourse, the tales open up space for their voices, and their language, to be heard. These are stories told and shared so that people will listen to a new discourse, but above all, they give voice to refugees who can ultimately talk about their no-win situations to listeners who have ears to hear and willingness to transmit that experience without distortion or prejudice.

The "Refugee Tales" Project: how it works

> *You were transported in a wooden vessel across a broad expanse of water to a place which rendered your tongue silent. Look. Listen. Learn. And as you began to speak, you remembered fragments of a former life. Shards of memory. […] You dressed your fractured memory in the strange words of the new country* (Phillips 2001, pp. 220–1).

Present-day migrations are often characterised by political and/or economic crises occurring as a direct result of colonial rule, neo-colonialism, or decolonisation. For the reasons specified, it may be argued that feelings of displacement and discontinuities, already experienced by human beings who unwillingly and forcibly took part in the Atlantic slave trade, are still experienced by contemporary migrants upon arriving at Western, 'civilized' countries. Although not uprooted, if contemporary migrants after a perilous, long journey manage to reach a Western society, that most of the time "colonized [and] plunder[ed] for centuries" (Metha 2019, p. 3) their countries of origin, already upon their arrival they are regarded as unwelcomed outsiders. Furthermore, the imperative forms of "Look. Listen. Learn." employed by Phillips to describe the senses of displacement and discontinuities felt by uprooted human beings who were allocated to overseas lands intended to be capitalized on by colonizers, represent, at the present time, three of the numerous key words that characterise the "Refugee Tales" project as it will be explored later in this section.

At a time when global culture, highly developed technologies and general freedom of movement characterise Western societies, paradoxically, borders are being redefined, reinforced and sometimes militarized; cross border and international circulation intensifies and simultaneously becomes more complex, creating mixed, transitional, and pending statuses that impact people's destinies (Anderson 2014, p. 4). Under these circumstances, unrestricted travel across borders is granted to individuals – passport owners – who can prove their status as legitimate, Western citizens. The frontier area separating political jurisdictions or geographic regions functions as a sorting zone in which the identifying characteristics of a region disappear to let the differentiating ones take over. Thomas Nail broaches a variant definition of border. To Nail, borders can be understood as a system that appears to be stable, but it can undergo a rapid change if somehow disarranged:

> For me, a border is a process that modulates the circulation of things. It continually distributes and redistributes flows of movement that pass through or around it. [...] The border is a process in the sense that it is a metastable state. Just like a vortex, it requires a constant supply of energy input to maintain its form. Borders, political and psychological, are always eroding in various ways and have to be repaired, reformed, and refortified. [...] The border is the process of continual repair, maintenance, and defense. Even when people or things pass across the border undetected their status on the other side changes. [...] When [people across borders illegally] they are criminalized for it and begin to circulate inside a world of detention centers, private deportation industries, immigration enforcement raids, and capitalist exploitation. The border is not just at the limit of society, but borders are like webs that weave through all society. For an illegal border crosser, the border inside a country is anywhere where one can be reported and removed (Nail 2022, p. 2).

Detaining foreign nationals for the purpose of immigration control is a practice that has a long history and undoubtedly characterises those societies with growing economy. However, in our globalised world, where distances can be shortened, features of motion and mobility are rather a privilege granted to the rich countries and their peoples rather than the whole worldwide community. We live in "bordered world" (Herd 2021, p. 149) and as put forth by Nail "the border is not just at the limit of society, but borders are like webs that weave through all society" (2022, p. 2) and these in return render access to countries for individuals without the right documents difficult if not unachievable. On the contrary, undocumented individuals who manage to cross frontier areas relying on human being traffickers or on long improvised journeys then "the border inside a country is anywhere where one can be reported and removed" (Nail 2022, p. 2). This is the exact scenario developed by Conservatives in the United Kingdom over the last two decades.

On May 25, 2012, "The Telegraph" – a national British daily broadsheet newspaper – published an article titled: *Theresa May interview: 'We're going to give illegal migrants a really hostile reception'*. In conversation with James Kirkup, Theresa May clearly stated her government position on the issue of migration summarising it in a phrase coined for the occasion: "hostile environment". In point of fact, she introduced the "Hostile Environment Policy", that is to say a set of administrative and legislative measures designed to make staying in the United Kingdom as difficult as possible for illegal immigrants. Five years later, in August 2017, her announcement "was chosen as one of her most powerful quotes" as emphasised by Amelia Hill in her article for the British daily newspaper "The Guardian":

> 'Hostile environment': the hardline Home Office policy [...] It is a boast that Theresa May has been repeating for the past five years. "The aim is to create, here in Britain, a really hostile environment for illegal immigrants," she said in 2012 when, as home secretary, she was challenged on why annual net immigration, then running at about 250,000, was stubbornly above the Conservatives' controversial "tens of thousands" target. It was, the Telegraph noted, a rare moment when a politician who otherwise chose her language with "feline delicacy", avoiding "a few stray words or a rash promise", allowed it to become "uncharacteristically vivid". Despite her "safety-first" approach to public statements, May obviously liked that vividness. She has taken to repeating the phrase on demand. In August, it was chosen as one of her most powerful quotes. [...] "The Conservatives seem hellbent on creating a hostile environment for anyone not from the UK," says the Liberal Democrat home affairs spokesman Ed Davey. "These scare tactics should be beneath any civilised government." (Hill 2017, online edition)

Nonetheless, Conservatives has managed to create a hostile environment: the number of Detention Immigration Removal Centres scattered across the United Kingdom land (some are located near international airports) as well as the number of detainees have increased over the last years. Figures and data are available at https://aviddetention.org.uk/welcome-avid, a "network of voluntary organisations providing support for people in detention" whose website can also be accessed clicking the link within the Gatwick Detainees Welfare Group website. A further evidence of the "Hostile Environment Policy" is provided by a video uploaded on the Internet free platform of YouTube in 2019 by Detention Action group. Over a span of five minutes and forty-four seconds, Bella Sankey – director of Detention Action – brings the "Indefinite Detention Scandal" to viewers' attention. Among data, figures and statements, it is shown a disconcerting shot of a mobile billboard truck that reads:

> In the UK illegally? Go home or face arrest. Text HOME to 78070 for free advice, and help with travel documents. We can help you to return home voluntarily without fear of arrest or detention. www.promogroup.co.uk 020 7978 6399 (The Indefinite Detention Scandal 2019, 03'08").

On that note, Herd's and Pincus's proactive engagement in the "Refugee Tales" project is undisputedly needful and essential for just, unbiased and above all welcoming Western societies, and the purposes toward which the founders' efforts are directed are crystal clear in the following quote:

> Founded in 2014 by Gatwick Detainees Welfare Group, Refugee Tales is a civil society project that calls attention to the fact that the UK is the only country in Europe that detains people indefinitely under immigration rules, and which in so doing calls for that policy to end. The way the project makes its call is by sharing the stories of people who have experienced detention, and the way it shares those stories is in the context of a public walk (Herd 2019, p. 15).

On "13th-21st June, 2015" the very first "public walk" took place "from Dover to Crawley via Canterbury". Initially, the project was conferred with the subtitle "A Walk in Solidarity with Refugees, Asylum Seekers and Detainees" (Herd 2016, p. 133), and for an educated audience, the name of the project and, to a certain degree its subtitle, are a reminder of one of the English canonical literary works:

> Drawing inspiration from Chaucer's *Canterbury Tales*, the project, which aims to raise awareness on indefinite immigration detention in the UK and reclaim its abolition, summons and combines the world-making power of storytelling and the extraordinary bonding potential of walking in solidarity to reconfigure the English polity as a welcoming space of listening and 'appearance' (De Michelis 2019, p. 27).

Allegedly, the greatest contribution of *The Canterbury Tales* – written between 1387 and 1400 – to English literature was the act of making the use of the English vernacular in mainstream literature attractive to general public, as opposed to French, Italian or Latin widely employed at that times in scientific and literary written productions (Dabbeni 2004, p. 29). In point of fact, another analogy with Geoffrey Chaucer's collection of stories lays in the use of contemporary non-standard English, as migrants and refugees are not a monolithic group. It has to keep in mind that they originate from many regions and speak different languages. Notwithstanding that, in the moment they face detention, they become a homogenous group: they have to speak and engage in the official language of the hostile environment, and, for the majority of them, English is their second language. Then, following Chaucer's pattern, as Herd states in the "Afterword" in the first published volume, the project has "Three fundamental elements: a culturally charged sense of space, the visible fact of human movement, and an exchange of information through the act of telling stories" (2016, p. 133). The latter allows individuals' reminiscences to emerge and be uttered, even though this develops into a means of "dress[ing their] fractured memory in the strange words of the new country" (Phillips 2001, p. 221). Nevertheless, as De Michelis points out,

> the Refugee Tales project provides a forceful antidote. In its triple capacity as oral storytelling, written word and movement in space, the project is meant to heal and restore the very connective tissue which may help making up a new, and 'humane', shared imaginary of openness, respect and relationality, and aims to leave a mark on the discursive and cultural geography of the nation (2019, p. 31).

Although painful and difficult, the possibility of telling anecdotes, life experiences, accounts of event spontaneously and at the individual's pace may represent a way "to reconfigure the English polity as a welcoming space of listening and 'appearance'" (De Michelis 2019, p. 27) and "the result is a space in which stories circulate and re-circulate, told and heard in such a way that they become the basis of the collective's experience" (Herd 2019, p. 21), that is to say a community of walkers who comes out into the open and shares a free, borderless space:

> And what comes out of Southwark / it is a whole new language / Of travel and assembly and curiosity / and welcome. / To make his English sweete. / That's why Chaucer told his tales. / How badly we need English / To be made sweet again / Rendered hostile by act of law / So that even friendship is barely possible (Herd 2016, pp. viii-ix).

The above quotation is an extract from Herd's prologue written for the first published volume. Herd – poet, professor of modern literature and activist – wrote three prologues and one epilogue emulating some of Chaucer's use of the elements of poetry that include structure, form, speaker, figurative language, meter, theme, tone, syntax, and diction because "Chaucer inscribes into the language (which he was helping to create) a deep connection between poetry and human movement" (Herd 2015, online publication). That being said, already in the first stanza of the first prologue, despite of the style of the written production, Herd specifies:

> This is not a poem / It is an act of welcome / It announces / That people present / Reject the terms / of a debate that criminalises / Human movement / It is a declaration / This night in Sheperdswell / Of solidarity (Herd 2016, p. v).

The above stanza may be read as the "Refugee Tales" statute delivered as a poetic document that sets forth the activist and welcoming nature of the project, a project that: a) stands out against the "Hostile Environment Policy" introduced by Theresa May; b) emphasises the significant and fitting relationship between literature and "human movement"; c) corroborates and pursues Chaucer's attempt to create a new language able to reach a general public in order "To make his English sweete. / [as] / we need English / To be made sweet again".

As literature reveals the human history and the project is about how human nature is, in a podcast about the issue of migration in the United Kingdom, Ali Smith (one of the famous writers who recounted the stories of human beings caught up in the UK immigration system) states that "stories are welcoming in and walking alongside" (2016, 00:57–01:00). She goes on quoting John Berger and his reflection on the role of the storyteller: "I have been thinking about the storyteller's responsibility to be hospitable, you invite someone into a story, you must look after at the person who is listening to you and you must also ensure the person's ears are open because hospitality goes two ways" (2016, 03:08–03:27). The storytelling that occurs during the walk is also an act of hospitality. The impromptu storyteller who can eventually walk free on the English land and cross, although local, boundaries releases thoughts, feelings and reminiscences of his past and present life. In doing so, the impromptu storyteller invites the audience to enter his world and to know about himself. What Herd defines also as "an exchange of information" turns into a trust-based relationship between the teller and the listener. Walter Benjamin in his essay "The Storyteller Reflections on the Works of Nikolai Leskov" (1936) exploring the art and practice of storytelling provides a definition that perfectly fits the walks of solidarity's purposes:

> Experience which is passed on from mouth to mouth is the source from which all storytellers have drawn. And among those who have written down the tales, it is the great ones whose written version differs least from the speech of the many nameless storytellers. Incidentally, among the last named there are two groups which, to be sure, overlap in many ways. And the figure of the storyteller gets its full corporeality only for the one who can picture them both. When someone goes on a trip, he has something to tell about (Benjamin 1936, p. 83).

The act of storytelling that takes place during the annual walks "is not a filtering, it is a collaboration" (Herd 2016, 07:00) and above all it confers agency and visibility to "nameless storytellers" who still remain anonymous but, on this occasion, they feel free to express themselves without the pressure of answering correctly to the many and redundant questions made by Home Officers.

In 1992, Marc Augé coined the neologism "non-places" or anthropological spaces of transience where human beings remain anonymous, and that do not hold enough significance to be regarded as "places" in their anthropological definition, i.e. places characterised by an ideal balance between spatial arrangement and societal organization. The anthropologist considers refugee camps and "extended transit camps where the planet's refugees are parked" (1995, 33–34) as non-places. Thirty years later, Detention Immigration Removal Centres can be regarded as non-places. They are not encrusted with historical meaning and creative of social life. As put forth by Augé, these are places that cannot be defined as relational, historical, or concerned with identity. An example is provided in "The Observer's Tale" as told by N:

> The first days of my life here were spent trying to find a reason to be detained.
> I didn't have a motive for going to the bathroom. Even if I had, I had no clothes to change into.
> They just gave me a set of black undergarments. Just wearing these degrading clothes, my senses of helplessness was greater. Now it is around a week that I have been detained. Somebody is looking for me with a file, as today the caseworker talked with me. Perhaps I am being released.
> Somebody is translating his words – 'This place was just temporary, now we are going to move you to the permanent wing.'
>
> It is a bitter news.
> I say to myself –
> 'Every day is worse than the one before.'
>
> I put my stuff in a rubbish bag and follow officers.
> After a complicated path, a small door opens into a huge space with three floors instead of two.
> More crowded (N 2019, pp. 125–126).

As we learn in the section "About the Contributors", N was given the refugee status in 2018 after two long years spent in detention. He is now a volunteer at the "Refugee Tales" project and, as it started in third volume, he is one of the few individuals who managed to write his own story. N's sentences are weighty and characterised by bewilderment: "trying to find a reason to be detained"; sense of vulnerability and depression detectable in the noun "helplessness"; sense of transient: moving from one centre to another; lack of space; sense of alienation. Furthermore, a clear evidence of homogenisation is given at the breakfast table episode:

> Officers open the doors for the rooms for breakfast.
> I am looking at other detainees to know what to do.

> Everyone has a plastic container in their hand.
> Downstairs, down the staircase.
> People with different shapes and nationalities, but the dishes are all the same colour.
> Some are walking loose along the wing, as if eating takes their energy (N 2019, p. 124).

Having breakfast, or simply sitting at a table and have dinner with other human beings, should be a moment of conviviality; on the contrary, it is depicted as an exhausting activity. Then, the contrast between different physical aspects and same dishes denotes carelessness. A multi-ethnic group should have been served with different dishes according to their dietary habits due to culture, ethical and moral values, religion, health issues. Furthermore, as in the previous extract, his sentences are concise, his thoughts mark discontinuity and the double space between reminiscences (in the previous extract) may indicate a break in the narration taken because of a sense of displacement. Whatever the circumstances, being held in prison-like conditions without a time limit causes anxiety and distress. Many people in detention already have traumatic backgrounds, and the psychological impact of being held is absolutely damaging. However, "there is a more general sense, less easy to capture in particular details, in which the person seeking asylum in the UK is locked out of the language." (Herd 2017, p. 118) In these non-places the official language is the language of bureaucracy which is usually difficult to decipher for mother tongue individuals too. The repercussion, as Herd points out, "isn't metaphorical, the language is the border. It isn't the whole border, nor its most manifest aspect, but it is absolutely a medium in which the border takes effect" (Herd 2017, p. 120).

Conclusions

The "Refugee Tales" project comprises collections of tales published in textual editions alongside a politically embodied campaign to call for an end to the practice of indefinite detention of asylum seekers in the United Kingdom. The United Kingdom is the only country in Europe that detains people indefinitely for administrative purposes and without judicial oversight.

While the titles of the tales follow a Chaucerian format, neither the tellers nor the persons in the tales are modelled on specific Chaucerian characters. *Refugee Tales* denies the pleasure of spotting coded resemblances between Chaucer's taletellers and updated narrators. In *Refugee Tales*, the stories are too true and urgent for the game of allusion. This project is about activism, human rights, taking a stand, speaking up and giving a voice to those human beings who are marginalised and cannot make themselves visible. There are no names in the titles because it is simply too dangerous to put them in. Anonymity is vital.

Importantly, the writers or narrators are not listed as "authors" but as "contributors", always to emphasise the spirit of collaboration and accurateness in a welcoming and hospitable project. The majority of tales are "as told to", few tales are "as told by". The fourth annual walk, marks a relevant change, as some of the storytellers wrote their own story that were published in the third volume. This is a vivid indication of the strenuous work that has been done by Herd, Pincus and all the people who have been taking active part in the project along with the strenuous efforts to develop people's awareness of the "Hostile Environment Policy" introduced by Theresa May along with the proliferation of detestation centre on English land.

> Immigration detention is the practice of holding people who are subject to immigration control in custody, while they wait for permission to enter or before they are deported or removed from the country. It is an administrative process, not a criminal procedure. This means that migrants and undocumented people are detained at the decision of an immigration official, not a court or a judge. Unlike most other European countries, there is no time limit on immigration detention in the UK. Home Office policy says that detention must be used sparingly and for the shortest possible period. But in reality, many thousands are held each year, and some for very lengthy periods, causing serious mental distress. (http://www.aviddetention.org.uk/)

In 2020, due to the Covid-19 restrictions, the annual walk did not take place, but the organisers and volunteers did not give up "like all other large-scale public events, Refugee Tales 2020 had to be re-thought" (Herd 2021, p. 146). Internet and digital technologies allowed the walk to be dispersed: "instead of gathering in one location and collectively following a shared route, people walked where they could, drawn together across a three-day weekend by a series of online events: talks calling for A Future Without Detention" (Herd 2021, p. 146). At the end of the online event, as "the project plotted their location on an online map" (p. 146), the annual walk was done "in over twenty countries worldwide" (p. 146). In point of fact, the fourth volume is a collection of international tales. Furthermore, "the publication date of *Refugee Tales IV* marks a significant international anniversary [...] the Convention Relating to the Status of Refugees" (p. 149) signed in 1951. This document reasserted the values of human recognition and sanctioned refugees' rights and the international standards of treatment for their protection. The fourth volume brought to the surface the international scenario where too many countries continue to deny human rights and close their borders to "human movement", and the virtual walks allowed to make bridges across the world, as bridges can be crossed and the network of sharing stories along the way can be widened. On account of this, Herd in his fourth "Afterword" affirms the intention of pursuing Refugee Tales initial quest: "the act of sharing stories cannot stop. And nor can the walking because, as the project walks, so in walking, it looks to reclaim the ground. The ground is solidarity to which the sharing of stories is crucial. The walk continues. Detention must end" (Herd 2021, p. 152).

Works Cited

Augé, Marc: *Non-places Introduction to an Anthropology of Supermodernity.* trans. Howe, John, Verso, London-New York (1992) 1995.

Anderson, Ruben: *Illegality, Inc. Clandestine Migration and the Business of Bordering Europe.* University of California Press, Oakland California 2014.

Benjamin, Walter: *The Storyteller Reflections on the Works of Nikolai Leskov,* in "Illuminations", Harcourt Brace Jovanovich, New York (1936) 1968, pp. 83–109.

Dabbeni, Gianpaolo: *Influenze Latine Sulla Cultura dell'Inghilterra nel Medioevo.* in Bonvecchio, Dabbeni, Tonchia (eds.): "Aurea Latina Hereditas: Influenze latine nella cultura e nelle lingue europee. Come sopravvive il latino nel Friuli-Venezia-Giulia, in Alpe-Adria e in altre nazioni europee", EUT Edizioni Università di Trieste, Trieste 2004, pp. 25–47, https://www.openstarts.units.it/.

De Luca Picione, Raffaele et Al.: 'Borders, Movement, and Being-in-Between an interview with Thomas Nail', in: INTERNATIONAL JOURNAL OF PSYCHOANALYSIS AND EDUCATION: SUBJECT, ACTION & SOCIETY, 2022/II (2), pp. 2–6. DOI: https://doi.org/10.32111/SAS.2022.2.2.1.

De Michelis, Lidia Anna: 'Reclaiming Human Movement, Restor(y)ing Hope', in: FROM THE EUROPEAN SOUTH, 2019/5, pp. 27–42, https://www.fesjournal.eu/.

Herd, David and Pincus Anna (eds.): *Refugee Tales.* Comma Press, Manchester 2016.

Herd, David and Pincus Anna (eds.): *Refugee Tales II.* Comma Press, Manchester 2017.

Herd, David and Pincus Anna (eds.): *Refugee Tales III.* Comma Press, Manchester 2019.

Herd, David and Pincus Anna (eds.): *Refugee Tales IV.* Comma Press, Manchester 2021.

Herd, David: 'Calling for an End to Indefinite Detention: the Spatial Politics of Refugee Tales', in: FROM THE EUROPEAN SOUTH, 2019/5, pp. 15–25, https://www.fesjournal.eu/.

Landa, J.Á. García: 'Literature in Internet', in: Posteguillo, Santiago / Esteve, María José / Gea-Valor Lluïsa (eds.): *The Texture of Internet, Netlinguistics in Progress.* Cambridge Scholars Publishing, Newcastle 2007, pp. 143–159.

Metha, Suketu: *This Land is our Land an Immigrant's Manifesto.* Farrar Straus and Giroux, New York 2019.

Phillips, Caryl: 'Epilogue: Exodus', in: Phillips, Caryl: *The Atlantic Sound.* Vintage Random House, London 2001 [2000], pp. 214–221.

Phillips, Caryl: 'Introduction: A New World Order', in: Phillips, Caryl: *A New World Order – Selected Essays.* Secker & Warburg, London 2001, pp. 1–6.

Phillips, Caryl: 'A Life in Ten Chapters', in Phillips, Caryl: *Color Me English – Reflections on Migration and Belonging.* The New Press, New York, London 2011, pp. 107–112.

Websources

https://aviddetention.org.uk/welcome-avid (last access June 24, 2023).
https://detentionaction.org.uk/get-involved/end-indefinite-detention/ (last access June 24, 2023).
https://www.gdwg.org.uk/ (last access June 24, 2023).
https://migrationobservatory.ox.ac.uk/resources/briefings/immigration-detention-in-the-uk/ (last access June 15, 2023).
https://theconversation.com/modern-day-canterbury-tales-refreshes-chaucer-to-tell-the-lost-stories-of-refugees-42981 (last access June 15, 2023).
https://www.theguardian.com/books/audio/2016/jun/24/migration-ali-smith-david-herd-and-wolfgang-bauer-listen-for-the-true-story-books-podcast (last access May 31, 2023).
https://www.theguardian.com/uk-news/2017/nov/28/hostile-environment-the-hardline-home-office-policy-tearing-families-apart (last access May, 28, 2023).
https://www.telegraph.co.uk/news/uknews/immigration/9291483/Theresa-May-interview-Were-going-to-give-illegal-migrants-a-really-hostile-reception (last access May, 28, 2023).
https://www.unhcr.org/about-unhcr/who-we-are/1951-refugee-convention (last access June 24, 2023).

Paolo Caponi (University of Milano La Statale)

When Space Gets in the Way. The Suspension of Disbelief and "the best quality of life possible"

> I know thee not: what messenger art thou?
> *The Somonyng of Everyman* (anon.)

In the very famous late 15th-century morality play *The Somonyng of Everyman*, Death comes to Everyman and announces him it is time to die. Everyman asks for more time, even trying to bribe God's messenger. Death, who cares nothing about money, denies Everyman's last request, but will allow him to take a companion for his journey. The plethora of Everyman's friends and relatives (Fellowship, Kindred, Cousin, Goods, Wisdom, Confession, Beauty, Strength, Discretion, Five Wits…) promise to go anywhere with him, but as soon as they hear of the true nature of the journey, "all renne from me full fast" (Greg 1904, v. 844), Everyman says. Only Knowledge and Good Deeds do not abandon him. If, however, Good Deeds "wyll not forsake" him "indede", and even says "I wyll speke for thee" in front of "God moost mighty" (vv. 853; 874), the play strictly defines the role of Knowledge, who escorts Everyman to his deathbed but no further – reminding us, sadly enough, that things have not altered significantly since Medieval times in many respects.

Moralities like *Everyman* help us focus on the link between literature and other domains, namely the Medical Humanities and all the friends that accompany this discipline – not unreliable friends, however, as in the play, but most loyal ones. In this essay, the role of one of them – poetry, and the peculiar state of mind associate with its reading or writing – will be evaluated in the light of an innovative approach to therapy recently carried on by the Istituto Nazionale Tumori (henceforth, INT) in Milan (Veneroni et Al. 2018).

Lucia's dream

The "clinical" history of poetry, and its support to the process of inward healing, has long been recognized, even though it has always suffered from the merciless comparison with other arts like dance or drama, more physical and conjunctive, "more accessible and popular" (Longo 2008, p. 68). The esoteric, cryptic, even secretive features customarily associated with poetry, its "shadow of mysticism" (Longo 2008, p. 68), can be at the origin of its being "the slowest creative art to gain reputation for the healing and growth potential it possesses" (Kemplar 2003, p. 118). In addition, research into the impacts of poetry (for clinicians or patients) is limited, especially if compared with formal reviews of the state of narrative medicine (Kwok et Al. 2022, p. 92). Recently, however, the relation between poetry and medicine has gone through a general reconsideration, and this has implied not only a reassessment of the ways in which the poetic domain can be approached and explored with an healing intent, but also a rather polemical stance towards narrative medicine, seen as hegemonic and mandatory in its approach to well-being or even as something that has "overgrown its limits" (Bleakley / Neilson 2022, p. 34). The bone of contention seems to be, among other things, precisely the hegemony of narrative in the representation of suffering, a hegemony that imposes a linearity, and an order of precedence, to events and symptoms that reclaim an immanent significance. Implied by narration is a structuring arch, an artificial selection and processing of events that can present themselves simultaneously and/or stubbornly resist diachrony: "we point out that such events need not be framed as linear, progressive and temporal. Rather, they may display as nonlinear and complex, messy, sporadic, and place-based" (Bleakley / Neilson 2022, p. 34). Luckily enough, this is not the place where to fuel a debate over the most eligible friend of healing, even though the reference to space, as disjunctive from the notion of linearity implicit in the habitual anamnesis, is particularly relevant in that it alludes to a peculiar quality of poetry capable of opposing the traditional peak-and-denouement-pattern approach. In its essence, the revenge taken by space over time, *pace* Foucault, can also be related to different modalities of consciousness and experience, opening the door to "suspensive" levels of perception that can draw into a kind of alliance and complicity and resist diachrony by avoiding to re-affirm its own dogmatic, its own precisely dictatorial laws.

The issue of the quality of life for patients affected by cancer is delicate and difficult to approach, especially with those adolescents who have to face a terminal prognosis. Up to now, and odd as it may seem, there is no real consensus on the best approach to use in daily clinical practice with terminally ill adolescent patients, and this subject comprises only a small part of the current medical literature (Meaghann / Mack, 2017 p. e26570). Whether and how to tell a person who is terminally ill the truth about his/her condition is, naturally enough, problematic. In daily clinical practice, caregivers often find themselves between Scylla and Charybdis, between the imperative – imposed by the law – to inform the patient about his/her condition and the necessity to keep hope alive. A thoughtful introduction of the use of poetry in the hospitals, however, "can allow for the testing of hypotheses and for incremental quality improvement" (Kwok et

Al., p. 98). *Conditio sine qua non*, of course, is the logistical establishment of a "safe space", to be intended both physically and psychologically, as a "structured community, capable of fostering personal connection amidst [...] multiple element of diversity" (Kwok et Al., p. 98).

The experiment carried on by the INT comes from daily experience of clinical work carried out by a multidisciplinary team in a huge pediatric ward devoted to the cure of cancer in children and adolescents, and tackles the psychological mechanisms "which affect teenage patients with terminal cancer, in order to allow the best quality of life possible" (Veneroni et Al., p. 166). Notably, it is based on literary premises, and precisely on the Coleridgian "suspension of disbelief" as filtered through the contemporary achievements in neurosciences, neuro mechanisms and processes of estrangement (Veneroni et Al., p. 166). This practice – not to be forgotten, a palliative treatment – deliberately resumes a speculative vision of poetry and addresses poetry and its fictional import for their potential creative capability. Patients have been, to a certain extent, encouraged to project themselves onto alternative, different worlds or scenarios so as to detach themselves from their *status quo*, performing that arrest of critical thinking implied in the theoretical assumptions that structure Coleridge's discourse. Accordingly, and crucially, the interpretation of the young patients' dreams during their terminal phase has been carried out through parameters formed on the basis of the auto-healing intents related to this "suspensive" mode of approach to life and illness, rather than on proper, institutionalized clinical or psychoanalytical practices:

> I had a strange dream. [...] I dreamt that I was at my 18th birthday party. It was a fantastic party. I was dressed like a princess, in pale blue and white. Everyone was there, my parents, my brothers and sisters, my boyfriend, and all my friends. You doctors and nurses were there too, and all the other patients. Then, at some point I saw Claudia [a girl who had been with Lucia during numerous hospitalizations who had died not long beforehand]. Claudia looked lovely, but she was thin. I could see she was ill and she couldn't talk. In my dream, I knew perfectly well that Claudia was dead, that she couldn't be there. But this didn't worry me. At some point, Claudia got into a hot-air balloon that was there, still attached to the ground, but that I knew would soon fly away. Her parents asked me if I could go with her because they didn't want her to leave alone. I really didn't want to leave the party, which was still in full swing. I was having a great time, and everyone was there for me. But, at the same time, I didn't want to leave Claudia alone. So I decided to go with her in the balloon. At some point, the balloon became detached from the ground and I began to rise up into the sky, higher and higher. I could see the party and my friends and family from above. I wasn't frightened, not at all, but I was very sorry to leave the people and the party behind. I already felt the loss. There was so much melancholy in my heart. I was sad, not frightened. I think this dream meant to say that I can feel free to fly, to become light, freed of the weight of this difficult time, and even free to choose (Veneroni et Al., p. 166).

Lucia was seventeen and had a soft tissue sarcoma with metastases to the lung, which was progressing and was also refractory to therapy. Lucia's dream introduces the complex topic of how adolescent patients adapt to the terminal stage of their disease. The therapeutic approach opted then for a suspension of rational judgment, refraining from any canonical interpretation (of the dream, in this case) that might have shed too much light, establishing a kind of therapeutic alliance based on assumptions that may remind us of Wilfred Bion's concept of *pseudos*, where a mutually shared lie in a dyadic relation functions as a protective strategy against outer menace and paranoia (Bion, 1997 (1963)).

So far, little is known about the psychological processes implemented by terminal patients to react and adapt to reality. Daily experience with Lucia and other patients has shown that the way in which adolescent patients adapt to a situation of terminality differs substantially from the adult or the elderly. Strange as it may sound, young people may often take an optimistic attitude to their clinical condition, still trusting in the future, leaving scarce space to the standardized practices adopted for adults (avoiding, for instance, the so-called EOD or "end of life discussions" (Veneroni et Al., p. 166)). Illusory defenses can fence off the anguish induced by thoughts of dying and can disconnect, momentarily, from the external world. Dreams (and daydreams) can help in the development of such abortive illusions, enabling Lucia for instance to organize her birthday party (which she did actually attend), or plan a trip to the Caribbean (which she never took).[1]

Suspending disbelief

The implicit notion of a "suspension of disbelief" exerted by, or imposed to, a receptive audience was recognized in ancient times. Aristotle first explored this peculiar state of mind in its relation to the principles of theater: famously, the fascination of the scenes of death experienced by an audience can help them release emotional tension and anxieties (κάθαρσις, catharsis). The actual coinage of the phrase dates 1817, when Coleridge in his *Biographia Literaria* goes back to the times of "the plan of the *Lyrical Ballads*" when "it was agreed" with Wordsworth that Coleridge would be concerned with a "supernatural" kind of poetry implying a "willing suspension of disbelief" (Coleridge 1817, p. 208). Interestingly, this was equated by Coleridge to the very essence of "poetic faith", and the idea was that if a writer could manage to infuse a "human interest and a semblance of truth" in those "shadows of imagination", the reader would suspend judgement concerning the implausibility of the matter (Coleridge 1817,

---

[1] Carlo Alfredo Clerici, personal communication.

p. 208). Very likely, however, the phrase resulted not much from the vexed collaboration with Wordsworth, but from Coleridge's proficiency in philosophical sciences that led him to inquiry on the nature and origin of illusions. A regular attendant at the Bristol Pneumatic Institute – a research center established in 1799 by Dr. Thomas Beddoes to study the medical effects of gases –, Coleridge witnessed some instant recoveries operated by the mere power of suggestion (Guest-Gornall 1973, p. 336). Indeed, the width of Coleridge's interests, his habitual, life-long frequentation of doctors and medical circles, his interests in mesmerism and in the human mind and its behavior in sleep, and, last but not least, his having been "an object of concern to many doctors throughout his life" (Guest-Gornall 1973, p. 327),[2] can even prospect a new scenario where Wordsworth's notorious influence is downsized and placed along other sources of influence of a nature not strictly "poetic" or literary. Mesmerism, indeed, and all its spurious off-springs – table-turning and clairvoyance among them – was the fashion of the 1850s and connects three generations of Romantic poets from Coleridge to Browning via Shelley (Karlin 1989, p. 65). Notably, Shelley's "The Magnetic Lady to Her Patient" (1822) was based on his experience with Jane Williams in 1820 in Pisa, when he undertook mesmerism to avoid surgery for kidney stones (Stanbury 2012, p. 12). The great divide between science and the humanities is something relatively recent, dating approximatively the same period, and Coleridge is no exception in his conjunctive attitude between the two realms. Much before him, John Donne may be considered one of the founders of "autopathography" (Bleakley / Neilson 2022, p. 202), carefully recording the symptoms of his budding cancer. John Keats, Coleridge's younger colleague, registered as a student of medicine at London Guy's hospital, receiving in 1816 the apothecary's license, and attended the Physical Society at Guy's where Coleridge was also a regular speaker (Bleakley / Neilson 2022, p. 202). And not that the divide is to be intended exclusively between poetry and medicine: as every reader of *Treasure Island* (1883) remembers well, Dr. Livesey was "not a doctor only", but also "a magistrate" (Stevenson 1883, p. 7). Coleridge's regard for hypnosis and for the personal relation between practitioner and subject may be at the origin of his *idée fixe* about the need to withhold judgement as something useful both to mythopoesis and for the ups and downs of everyday life. This is something he returns to over and over again in his essays, notebooks and letters, besides the *Biographia Literaria*, and resounds in an early statement about

---

2 Coleridge's relation with medicine in general and with doctors in particular has been made the subject of various studies. A biographical approach is that of Guest-Gornall, op. cit., largely based on *The Life of Samuel Taylor Coleridge* by James Gillman (1838); focused on the concepts of health and illness in Coleridge's time is Wallen 2004, while Coleridge's ambivalent relation with the prevailing medical and philosophical theories of his time is in Vickers 2004; useful sideways references to Coleridge and the coeval medical practice are in Roe 2017.

opium made when he was only nineteen: "opium never used to have any disagreeable effects on me; but it has on many" (Guest-Gornall, p. 329). In particular, in the later 18th and early 19th centuries Coleridge entertained thick relationships with a number of physicians. One of them, Dr. James Gillmann, opened his door, literally and figuratively, for meetings of prominent professionals in his house that eventually became known as "Coleridge's Thursday evening class" (Guest-Gornall, p. 329), where, among other things, the guests would discuss their dreams in detail, as well as the dreams of famous people and those described in literature and in classical treatises (Ford 1999, p. 171).

Admittedly, in contemporary medical practice the suspension of disbelief has come to signify a variety of things, stretching itself enough to include approaching the patient "slantwise", with an eye "backstage" while "contemplating a complex case" (Bleakley / Nelson 2022, pp. 138–139) – very much reminiscent, incidentally, of Freud's *gleichschwebende Aufmerksamkeit* (fluctuating attention) and his warnings against clichéd, preconceived notions. And it is also in the very essence of poetry to disrupt familiar responses, to remove the "veil of familiarity" (Furniss / Bath 1996, p. 86). In spite of this proliferation of meanings, however, this suspensive mode of copying illness implies, as mentioned above, a (re)focusing on the contingencies of space against the tyranny of diachrony, the latter particularly felt in front of a severe prognosis. Nothing more than poetry can perhaps better enhance "a *phenomenology of space*" as opposed to the "*narrativism's phenomenology of time*" Bleakley / Neilson 2022, p. 122),[3] with the crucial exception of those narratives that deliberately dismantle the artifice of narration itself, like, for instance, Samuel Beckett's short prose and novels (Bleakley / Neilson 2022, p. 122). A willing suspension of disbelief may be perhaps the very first stage of a dissociation not only between time and space, but also between body and soul, something that Coleridge obtained possibly from mesmerism but also, and more dramatically, through opium. It his perhaps a consequence of opium withdrawal his collapsing in an inn when he was touring through the Scottish forts to Inverness in August 1803, to which a prolonged state of disembodiment followed and he felt as he "was acting out a sort of Ode to Solitude" (Holmes 1990, pp. 353–354). Coleridge was also interested in NDE (near-death experiences), and among the possible sources for *The Rime of the Ancient Mariner* (1798; 1817) one is related to John Newton's NDE on board of the Greyhound off the coast of Ireland, when he was delivered "out of horrid darkness, into the marvelous light of the gospel" (Martin 1949, p. 69). More rudimentarily, a hero from Samuel Beckett's gallery of solipsists, Murphy in the eponymous novel (1938), reaches a similar dissociative state by tying himself naked to a rocking-chair and pushing relentlessly to and fro: "it set him free in his

---

3 Emphasis in the original.

mind. [...] And life in his mind gave him pleasure, such pleasure that pleasure was not the word" (Beckett 1938, p. 8). Beckett's typically incapacitated or mutilated bodies live in a sort of a temporal, and spatial, vacuum where the spatial archetype possesses a material essence, but, at the same time, it deals ineluctably with an imaginative and symbolical dimension. Molloy, Malone and all the other sociopathic narrators in Beckett's prose, experience, and almost crave, a progressive physical dismembering that is precipitated by the act of narration itself, an idle occupation and "almost lifeless, like the teller" (Beckett 1955–1958, p. 174). In the told and re-told stories, time and space end up losing their typical, kinetic connection while the focus shifts to the act of mere uttering, *hic et nunc*, something that exists *per se* without any proximity to what is being said or to any principle of linearity. In such cases, space may become a "black void" (Beckett 1955–1958, [*The Unnamable*] p. 306), a defensive area almost entirely created by language – no longer an external feature but also a mental construction where experience and intention coalesce. "Perhaps after all I'm in a kind of vault and this space which I take to be the street in reality is no more than a wide trench or ditch with other vaults opening upon it" (Beckett 1955–1958, [*Malone Dies*] p. 212). Already object of scrutiny precisely for those *pseudos* modalities cited above that mark Hamm and Clov's toxic, double-bind relation in his 1957 play *Endgame* (Restivo 1991, pp. 30; 307; 348), Beckett remodeled throughout his career the same dynamics of splitting that he either envisaged in a single, haunted brain or in his typical *nec tecum nec sine te* relationship of his pseudocouples. It is a repetition compulsion that progressively detach the subject from the object of the narrative and that separates the speaker from the urgency of what is being said, a philosophy of repetition that draws Beckett's narrators close to the Ancient Mariner, his expiatory tale and to all the tales founded on kinetic references that are lost.

As the psychoanalyst and early discoverer of the repairing role of narration in *Healing Fiction* (1989), James Hillmann, noted from his deathbed, this state of severe dissociation is the one obtained by mystics or advocated by Hinduism – an ἀπάθεια, or blessed apathy, that is opened up by the physical event of dying, and that affords even to the layman an experience of inward depletion and of timeless vacuum (Hillmann 2011).

Back to Knowledge

The harsh reality of the progression of illness and of the perspective of death are certainly not modifiable by any kind of dialogue or writing. In fact, assistance to a dying patient can rarely be carried out through words (Clerici / Veneroni 2014, p. 179). Through the therapeutic relation, or alliance, it is however possible to change the meaning that patients and their relatives assign to illness. The "suspensive" role of illusions, dreams and daydreams, as they come out of the INT ongoing clinical practice, point to something more structured and innovative than the habitual fallback provided by traditional "occupational therapies". The effort to rekindle hope in spite of everything is something that seems particularly productive with adolescents, in order to preserve a positive mental approach that can enable them "to come to terms" (Veneroni et Al., p. 166) with their future. Cure can be seen, in this case, as a daily re-enacting of hope and something that enables a re-focusing on space against time, even if the space is the virtual one afforded by the net (Clerici / Veneroni 2014, p. 179).

Coleridge himself, "the sole unbusy thing" (v. 5) in front of nature, gave voice in his late poem "Work without Hope" (1825) to the imperative of finding "an object" for "Hope" (v. 14) even when hope is no longer possible, when every contribution to the cycle of nature seems hampered, interrupted or annihilated (Coleridge 1825, p. 383). It is precisely this act *malgré tout* that can give a sense to our existence, and help us find our place within the schemes of nature and assist us in the journey Everyman has to take. The problem, as Knowledge in in the play only knows too well, is to embark on such a journey all alone: "Nay yet I wyll not from hens departe / Tyll I se where ye shall be come" (Greg 1904, vv. 802–803). With Beauty, Strength, and Fellowship gone, it is still up to Knowledge to provide some company in their stead.

Works cited

Beckett, Samuel: Murphy. Grove Press, New York 2010 (1938).
Beckett, Samuel: Three Novels: Molloy; Malone Dies; The Unnamable. Grove Press, New York 2009 (1955–1958).
Bion, Wilfred Ruprecht: Taming Wild Thoughts. Karnac Books, London 1997 (1963).
Bleakley, Alan / Shane Neilson: Poetry in the Clinic: Towards a Lyrical Medicine. Routledge, London, New York 2022.
Coleridge, Samuel Taylor: Biographia Literaria, ed. by Adam Roberts, Edinburgh University Press, Edinburgh 2014 (1817).
Coleridge, Samuel Taylor: Complete Poems, ed. by Wiilliam Keach, Penguin, London 1997.
Clerici, Carlo Alfredo / Veneroni, Laura: La psicologia clinica in ospedale. Consulenza e modelli di intervento. Il Mulino, Bologna 2014.
Ford, Jennifer: 'Samuel Taylor Coleridge and the Pains of Sleep', in: HISTORY WORKSHOP JOURNAL 1999/48, pp. 169–186.
Furniss, Tom / Bath, Michael: Reading Poetry. An Introduction. Pearson, London 1996.
Greg, Walter Wilson (ed.): Everyman from the edition by John Skot. Uystpruyst, Louvain 1904.

Guest-Gornall, R.: 'Samuel Taylor Coleridge and the doctors', in: MEDICAL HISTORY 1973/ 17:4, pp. 327–342.

Hillmann, James: 'Sto morendo ma non potrei essere più impegnato a vivere. L'ultima intervista. Al capezzale dello psicoanalista che ha domato il dolore per ragionare sulla propria fine', in: TUTTOLIBRI 29th Oct 2011.

Holmes, Richard: Coleridge. Early Visions. Vickers. New York 1990 (1989).

Karlin, Daniel: 'Browning, Elizabeth Barrett, and 'Mesmerism'', in: VICTORIAN POETRY 1989/27, 3/4, pp. 65–77.

Kemplar, N.Z.: 'Finding our voice through poetry and psychotherapy', in: JOURNAL OF POETRY THERAPY 2003/16, 4, pp. 217–220.

Kwok, Ian / Redwing Keyssar Judith / Spitzer Lee / Kojimoto Gayle / Hauser Joshua / Ritchie Christine Seel / Rabow Michael: 'Poetry as a Healing Modality in Medicine: Current State and Common Structures for Implementation and Research', in: JOURNAL OF PAIN SYMPTOM MANAGE Aug. 2022/64, 2.

Martin, Bernard: The Ancient Mariner and the Authentic Narrative. William Heinemann, London 1949.

Meaghann, S. Weaver / Mack, Jennifer: 'Holding hope', in: PEDIATRIC BLOOD AND CANCER Sep. 2017/64, 9.

Roe, Nicholas (ed.): John Keats and the Medical Imagination. Palgrave, London 2017.

Restivo, Giuseppina: Le soglie del postmoderno: Finale di partita. Il Mulino, Bologna 1991.

Stanbury, P.: 'Reflections of Mesmerism in Literature', in: ANAESTH INTENSIVE CARE 2012/40, 1, pp. 10–17.

Stevenson, Robert Louis: *Treasure Island*, ed. by John Seelie, Penguin, London 2014 (1883).

Strozier, Anne / Carpenter Joyce E. (eds.): Introduction to Alternative and Complementary Therapies. Routledge, London 2008.

Veneroni Laura / Ferrari Andrea / Podda Marta / Proserpio Tullio / Pagani Bagliacca Elena / Massimino Maura / Clerici Carlo Alfredo: 'Sul Buon Uso delle Illusioni in Oncologia; Esperienze e Comunicazioni di Fine Vita in Pazienti Adolescenti', in: RECENTI PROGRESSI IN MEDICINA Mar. 2018-1/109, 3, pp. 166–173.

Veneroni Laura, Ferrari Andrea, Proserpio Tullio, Pagani Bagliacca Elena, Podda Marta, Massimino Maura, Clerici Carlo Alfredo: 'Dreams and Illusions in Adolescents with Terminal Cancer', in: TUMORI JOURNAL Dec. 2018-2/104, 6, pp. 413–414.

Vickers, Neil: Coleridge and the Doctors, 1795–1806. Oxford University Press, Oxford 2004.

Wallen, Martin: City of Health, Fields of Disease: Revolutions in the Poetry, Medicine and Philosophy of Romanticism. Ashgate, Aldershot 2004.